THE MISTLETOE MURDER CLUB

KATIE MARSH

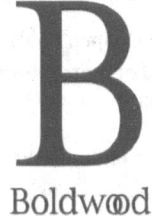

First published in Great Britain in 2025 by Boldwood Books Ltd.

Copyright © Katie Marsh, 2025

Cover Design by Head Design Ltd

Cover Images: Shutterstock

The moral right of Katie Marsh to be identified as the author of this work has been asserted in accordance with the Copyright, Designs and Patents Act 1988.

All rights reserved. No part of this book may be reproduced in any form or by any electronic or mechanical means, including information storage and retrieval systems, without written permission from the author, except for the use of brief quotations in a book review. This book is a work of fiction and, except in the case of historical fact, any resemblance to actual persons, living or dead, is purely coincidental.

Every effort has been made to obtain the necessary permissions with reference to copyright material, both illustrative and quoted. We apologise for any omissions in this respect and will be pleased to make the appropriate acknowledgements in any future edition.

A CIP catalogue record for this book is available from the British Library.

Paperback ISBN 978-1-83678-736-5

Large Print ISBN 978-1-83678-737-2

Hardback ISBN 978-1-83678-735-8

Trade Paperback ISBN 978-1-80635-315-6

Ebook ISBN 978-1-83678-738-9

Kindle ISBN 978-1-83678-739-6

Audio CD ISBN 978-1-83678-730-3

MP3 CD ISBN 978-1-83678-731-0

Digital audio download ISBN 978-1-83678-732-7

This book is printed on certified sustainable paper. Boldwood Books is dedicated to putting sustainability at the heart of our business. For more information please visit https://www.boldwoodbooks.com/about-us/sustainability/

Boldwood Books Ltd, 23 Bowerdean Street, London, SW6 3TN

www.boldwoodbooks.com

For Jo, with thanks for our WhatsApp chats of truth.

PROLOGUE

Beatrice Butler had come face to face with plenty of pistols in her time – but never one wrapped in mistletoe and tinsel. She stared down the barrel, which was shaking violently, as was the entire body of the person who appeared to want her dead.

Beatrice felt an unfamiliar pulse of fear as she sat on her chaise-longue at gunpoint. She may have underestimated the risks she was taking. She may have played with fire. She had assumed that her companion was too feeble, too lacking in backbone, and too stupid to ever confront her face to face. Then she felt relief washing through her. The weapon trained on her chest was a prop gun, not a real one. A Christmas cracker would be a more effective murder weapon than this.

The clock was ticking though, so it was time to move things along. This wasn't her time to die, not yet. When the stage legend that was Beatrice Butler shed her mortal coil, she wouldn't be doing so while wearing a fairy costume, her stage make-up only half done, her legacy not yet certain. No. She needed just a few more hours. One night to make stage history.

She stood up, smiling at her would-be killer, daring them to shoot. She used her most commanding tones, the rounded vowels that had captivated audiences around the world for the past fifty years. 'Don't be silly, now.' She held her hand out, her ruby ring sparkling. 'Give me the gun.'

'No.' The pistol was veering right and left now. Her attacker clearly believed it to be real. Beatrice saw the letters engraved on the barrel and her heart started to race. She hadn't been mistaken, had she? Her eyesight wasn't what it was.

Sweat dripped down the face of her assailant. 'You need to do what I tell you.'

Beatrice pulled herself up to her full height. 'I am Beatrice Butler. I never do what I am told.'

Then she lunged forward and reached for the gun.

ACT ONE

MURDER IN THE AIR

ONE DAY EARLIER

DRESS REHEARSAL

1

AMBER

Amber looked at the jumper and shook her head.

'No. I told you, I'm not wearing that. I wear black. Nothing but black.'

'But it's our first Christmas together!' Melissa, her half-sister, picked up a red sparkly jumper, which had Amber's name spelt out in holly leaves across the middle. 'And I've got a matching one!' She unbuttoned her silver puffa jacket. 'See?'

'It's still a no.' Amber folded her arms, increasing her pace as they neared the Beatrice Butler Theatre. The once-white facade Amber remembered from her youth was now a grimy grey, and the lights around the battered double doors were either smashed or flickering in quiet desperation. The theatre had been closed for the past year, but was reopening for one final Christmas show: *Jack and the Beanstalk*. Dame Beatrice Butler herself was coming out of retirement to lead the week-long production, and the press were going wild.

'You're no fun.' Melissa put the jumper back into her huge red 'Cool Yule' tote bag. 'Where's your festive spirit?'

'I told you. I don't have any.' Amber tried one of the glass-panelled doors, only to find it locked.

Melissa rolled her eyes. 'Then I am going to have to show you how to get your Christmas on.' She dug into her bag again, producing a Santa hat. 'How about wearing this instead?'

'No!'

'OK, then.' Another rummage. This time Melissa was waving an elf hat with pink sparkly ears.

Amber held up a hand. 'Please stop.'

'Honey.' Melissa put her hands on her hips. 'I'm from the US of A. I don't know how to stop. And, like it or not, you have actual family at Christmas, for the first time ever, and I'm not going to let you Grinch your way out of it.'

'Well, good luck with that.' Amber tried another door which opened with an ominous creak and they walked inside. The theatre foyer looked anything but ready to host an audience tomorrow night. A dusty chandelier above them looked as if it was hanging on by a thread and the worn red carpet was covered with brown stains. 'Clio and the rest of the cast must be in the auditorium – I think it's the dress rehearsal today.'

'So...' Melissa followed Amber as she made her way down some shallow steps towards the entrance to the stalls. 'Why am I here, again?'

Amber held open a heavy fire door and Melissa marched through. 'Clio says they need some publicity pictures. She thought you might be able to get some chat going on social media.' In reality, her best friend had come round to Amber's static caravan last night, a distance of about ten metres from her own, and begged her to bring Melissa to take some publicity pictures 'because Beatrice made the photographer cry and he quit.'

'She did, huh?' Melissa gave Amber a sideways glance. 'At least one of you appreciates my efforts. You know the reason you're so busy at your detective agency is down to me, don't you?'

'Actually, it's down to hard work and a great team.'

'True.' Melissa nodded. 'But it's thanks to me and my amazing socials that anyone knows how good you are.'

Amber bristled.

Melissa wisely changed the subject. 'So. Tell me about this pantomime thing, again? Another weird British Christmas tradition, right? Give me the lowdown.'

'Um...' Amber wondered where to start. She had watched her best friend Clio in various amateur pantomimes over the years, yet still she would still struggle to sum it up.

'OK.' She dropped her voice as they entered the long corridor that eventually led to the seats nearest the stage. 'So. A pantomime is a Christmas show.'

Melissa nodded. 'Like a nativity play?'

'No.'

'Huh.' Melissa thought for a moment, then her face lit up again. 'So is it about Santa?'

Amber shook her head. 'No. Pantomimes are always based on fairy tales.'

'What's Christmassy about fairy tales?'

Amber shrugged. 'I... I don't know.' She decided to plough on. 'But the female lead role – the Dame – is played by a man.'

'Uh-huh.'

'And Jack, the boy lead, he's played by a young woman in tights.'

Melissa snorted. 'Of course he is.'

'And there's almost always a Prince Charming.'

'Played by a woman?'

'Nope.' Amber shook her head. 'A man. In this case, Clio's childhood crush, Dexter Buchanan. He was in *EastEnders*, you know.'

'What's that?'

Amber was sweating slightly. 'It's a big UK show about – um, a market, in a square, in east London.'

'Sounds riveting.' Melissa's brow was furrowed. She rallied, listing things out on her fingers. 'OK, then. So we have gender-swapping, fairy tales...'

'Oh, and there's always a pantomime animal.'

'Played by...?'

'Humans, of course!' Amber smiled hopefully.

Melissa gave a sarcastic smile. 'Of course it is.'

'Oh, and there are songs and dances, and pies in the face, and *"it's behind you"*, and *"oh, no it isn't"*, and...'

'Oh, no what isn't?' Melissa looked utterly blank.

Amber stopped, biting her lip. How did you explain pantomime?

Melissa grimaced. 'I'm getting the same feeling I got about cricket. And baked beans.' She shook her head. 'Maybe I just need to see it in action.' She came to a halt, listening. 'Is that part of the show, or is that someone having a moment?'

Amber stopped too. They were next to the ladies' loos, and someone was definitely raising their voice in there. The plummy tone seemed familiar.

'I've told you already that I will never give up! You can do whatever you want to try to stop me, but you'll regret it! Just you see if you don't!'

It was Beatrice Butler, Amber was sure of it. Beatrice Butler in a very bad mood.

Melissa leant towards Amber, speaking in a whisper that could probably be heard in London. 'She must be talking into a mobile phone.'

Amber nodded. 'Thanks, I've worked that one out.'

'Rude.' Melissa flung her a wounded glance. 'I was just trying to be helpful.'

'I'm not going to let it go! I'm coming for you!' Footsteps approached the toilet door and both Amber and Melissa quickly ran on and opened the door into the theatre.

'They're over there.' Amber pointed towards the stalls. She wanted to double back and see who had been so angry. 'I've got to get to a client, but there's Clio – she'll tell you everything you need to know.'

Melissa's voice followed her as she walked away. 'There's no escaping Christmas, Amber! You can run but you can't hide!'

Amber ran back to the loos, but whoever had been inside had disappeared. Just to reassure herself she checked all the cubicles, but there was nobody there. Then she walked towards the exit, admonishing herself. This was a Christmas show. She didn't need to be a detective. Here, she could relax.

She looked down and saw a grinning toy elf in a green jerkin sticking out of her bag. Her phone bleeped. A text. From Melissa.

Told you so!

Amber grimaced and marched back out into the street, leaving the crumbling theatre behind her. That was her best friend Clio's world. Amber was happier when she could blend into the crowd, keep tabs on a mark or work out at the gym. She would go and see her new client. A nice relaxing Christmas dealing with unfaithful husbands or fraudulent co-workers, that was all Amber wanted. No murder investigations, no drama, just Amber and her two best friends making her detective agency a success.

Melissa wasn't going to change that.

Not in a million years.

Bah humbug.

2

CLIO

The cast of the Sunshine Sands' annual Christmas pantomime were only an hour into their final dress rehearsal and already there was murder in the air.

The two halves of the pantomime cow – assistant director Jaxon and costume designer Sylvia – had been immersed in the death throes of their exceedingly messy break-up ever since they had arrived in the theatre. As a result, screams had erupted from inside Daisy the Cow's body within moments of her first entrance in Act One, Scene One, and the poor animal currently looked as if she was having some kind of epileptic fit. Her mangy black and white ears thrashed as 'I hate you' came from her front half, only to be met with an epic shriek from the front end, preceded by what looked like a very hard shove. Daisy's forelegs shot forwards, cannoning into local 'celebrity' Dexter Buchanan, as he forgot his line for the third time. Given that said line was 'She's behind you,' the members of the cast who were watching were struggling not to groan.

Melissa took a break from taking pictures and tapped Clio on the shoulder. 'Isn't that guy a bit old to be playing Prince Charming?'

'You bet he is.' Ross Jones, aka Dame Trot, sat back down in his seat, leant over and tried to help himself to another one of Clio's toffees. 'I don't know why I bothered coming back from the loo. This is going to be a total disaster.'

Clio whipped the bag away and offered him a mince pie instead. She had decided to take up baking the week before, after yet another romantic liaison had come to an abrupt end. 'Pastry can't let me down,' she had muttered to herself, as she kneaded butter and flour in the tiny kitchen in her static caravan.

Ross abruptly withdrew his hand, flicking a crumb off the scarlet tights that were part of his costume. 'No thank you, darling. I'm not really one for mince pies.'

Clio turned on him. 'I saw you eating three of them yesterday, right from the Tesco Finest box!'

'Yes. Well.' She saw his skin flush. 'That's different. Yours are just a bit...'

Clio looked down at the fruits of her labour. They were fine, weren't they? Round. Baked. Pie-like. 'A bit what?'

'Well.' Ross gave an apologetic shrug. 'If you dropped one on your foot, bones would break, darling. My veneers can't take the chance.'

Clio opened her mouth to protest, but then remembered the way that her two best friends, Amber and Jeanie, had chosen to take theirs home, rather than eating them in front of her. She reached a finger out to prod one and nearly broke a nail.

Fine. She settled back in her seat, folding her arms. While everyone else in the world found solace in baking, she was obviously destined to fail at that as well. And now, here she was, about to take to the stage... in what was certainly going to be the worst pantomime the world had ever known.

Melissa leant forwards again. Clio was starting to regret asking Amber's half-sister to take publicity shots. She was developing a headache from all the questions.

'So why did Beatrice cast Dexter?'

'Good question.' Ross giggled. 'Maybe to make herself look good?'

Melissa gave a low laugh. 'And Beatrice Butler, she's like super-famous, isn't she? I mean, even I've heard of her. So why is she doing a Christmas pantomime for her big comeback? Why not – I don't know – a Shakespeare play or something?'

'Oh, that's easy, darling.' Ross nodded. 'Beatrice's late husband, Florian Followes, was a panto nut. It's how they met. He was Prince Charming and Beatrice was Jack. So this is coming full circle, or something like it, for her. And it's the last show in her theatre, before it closes its doors for ever. Rather sweet really, honouring him like that.' Ross checked his watch, which was much more flashy than the one he normally wore. 'God, we're going to be here for ever, aren't we?'

'Yes.' Onstage, Dexter was still struggling, and Clio found herself wondering why Beatrice had cast him. The two of them had starred in a long-running ITV series back in the day, so maybe that was something to do with it. And he had been a great actor once. Even two weeks ago he had been a lot more convincing than he was now. Perhaps something had happened to put him off his game. Whatever it was, Clio hoped he could get over it before opening night tomorrow. Beatrice had kept the cast small for her final production – choosing old acquaintances like Ross and Clio, who had both been in every Sunshine Sands amateur dramatic society production since time began. Dexter was the only newbie. Clio asked herself why.

Given the nightmare unfolding onstage, Clio – watching Dexter as Prince Charming struggle through his lines – couldn't help feeling it wasn't such a bad thing that she hadn't landed the leading part she had once wanted. Instead, she was playing Blackheart, the evil giant Blunderbore's henchman. When she had auditioned, part of her had hoped that she might get to play Fairy Moonshine, only to realise that Beatrice Butler had inevitably marked this part out for herself. As Dexter missed a line for the fourth time, Clio heard a loud sigh from the seat next to her, so gusty that it rippled the surface of her steaming mug of tea.

'Honestly. Why don't we just put Dexter out of his misery? Get in a drama student to play Prince Charming? At least they'd be the right age.' Ross rolled his eyes with considerably more dramatic verve than Dexter was displaying on stage. He leant towards Clio, finely plucked eyebrows arched beneath his receding hairline, speaking in the loudest stage whisper Clio had ever heard. 'Have you seen the size of his face on the posters? It's obscene.'

Clio shrugged, trying to keep her expression non-committal. The fact was that Dexter had once been famous enough to be one of the posters on teenage Clio's wall. As she had been busy dodging PE and getting crushes on wildly inappropriate men, Dexter had even been famous enough to grace the cover of *GQ* and to be 'Bum of the Month' in *Heat* magazine. Back then no red carpet and no movie premiere had been complete without Dexter Buchanan and his trademark brown quiff, tight jeans, Marlboro Reds and mahogany spray tan. After moving on from a five-year stint in *EastEnders*, he had joined the cast of *Hollyoaks* only for Hollywood to come calling. He had jetted out at some point around 2010, all signed up to play a superhero, saying in every news outlet possible that he would never be coming back.

Sadly, Hollywood had not seen his career the same way, and he had slunk back a few years ago and gone to ground. A few parts appeared here and there, of diminishing length, but these days, Dexter's beautifully capped teeth had more star quality than he did. Now he was reduced to switching on the Sunshine Sands Christmas lights and scraping a living playing roles like 'sinister stalker' in *Crimestoppers* ads. When Clio had started rehearsal, she had been a little bit in love with Dexter, her teenage self impossibly impressed that she would be sharing a stage with the man she had once practised kissing on, in poster form. She had approached their first rehearsal together with all the fizzing excitement she had brought to her first Take That concert, excited to be in a room with him, even wondering if a spark might ignite between them. After a moderately successful start to rehearsals, he slumped, and now Clio saw that Dexter was being outperformed by absolutely everybody and everything onstage, including Daisy the Cow's udders.

Despite Dexter's inability to remember cues, hit his mark, or even master the simplest chase scenes – always managing to end up front and centre – Clio had still tried to be kind, showing solidarity with a fellow actor. Last week she had offered to take him to the pub to run his lines, something she categorically did not have time for given how much overtime she was doing at the detective agency at the moment. However, in response, Dexter had simply run a hand through his hair transplant and claimed that he had everything under control, and that he was in the running for a huge Netflix series, with the contract due to come through 'any week now, yeah, yeah, it's going to be huge.' That night he had promptly gone off and snogged Kylie Silver, the wide-eyed twenty-year-old playing Jack, underneath the plastic mistletoe at the local pub.

Ross sniggered as Dexter consulted his script again. 'God, I feel like this production may actually be the death of someone before the run is out.'

Clio knew what he meant. She looked around the dilapidated theatre, wondering if the dusty chandelier above her would even make it through the run. She sank even further backwards and her worn red velvet seat creaked beneath her. The Beatrice Butler Theatre had opened in the late 1800s, as Her Majesty's Theatre, back when the seaside town of Sunshine Sands had been a mecca for Victorian high society, attracting the great and the good to bathe in its supposedly healing waters. Now, Clio's home was largely famous for winning the dubious title of England's rainiest seaside town. The theatre was fading gently, along with the pier next door, and today the interior was looking as old as Clio felt. Cream paint flaked from the damp walls, the stage creaked, and the thick maroon curtains were fraying at the edges.

Sighing, Clio reached into her bag, pulling out the jar of Nutella that Jeanie had placed in there only yesterday. Taped to it was a spoon and a note, 'Rehearsal fuel – enjoy', in Jeanie's rounded script.

She dug the spoon deep into the jar, pulling it out and planting it into her mouth, sighing with satisfaction. 'Can I have some?' Ross eyed her hopefully. He dug around in his rucksack and Clio caught sight of something glinting. 'I have some baguette to go with?'

'Absolutely not.' Clio dug the spoon in again. 'And what is that?' She reached down and pulled a shiny A4 envelope out of Ross's bag. 'Oh my God, Ross! Did you get it?'

'Well...' Ross flushed, his eyes lowered.

'But you said it cost too much!'

'What can I say?' Ross smiled. 'I had a good week!'

'An original script for *Singin' in the Rain*.' Clio stroked the envelope reverently. 'Can I open it?'

'No.' Ross held out his hand for the envelope. 'Signed by all the leads.' His eyes were alight. 'I can't believe I got hold of it.'

'Good for you. Did you sell a mansion, or something?' Clio nudged him.

'Something like that.' Ross tucked the envelope back into his bag. His collection of theatre memorabilia was huge: everything from costumes to programmes to vinyl cast albums. It was very helpful when she had to dress up for parties. Which was rare, now she was in her mid-forties, but still.

'Where do you think Beatrice Butler is?' Melissa and her questions again. 'It would be neat to have some shots of her in action.'

Ross pulled a face. 'Depends what action you're talking about. She can be a one-woman hit squad. She normally sits there at that big desk in the central aisle, waiting to kill any performer unlucky enough to be onstage. If she was here, even those teenage dancers over there...' He gestured towards the Sunshine Sizzlers who were dressed as Magic Beans for their opening number and had colonised the front left side of the stalls. 'Even they would stop taking selfies and doing their fancy TikToks. They wouldn't dare.'

Melissa frowned. 'So if she's such a cow, why are you all doing this?'

Clio and Ross glanced at each other, laughing.

Ross rolled his eyes. 'Because we've been in the panto every year, darling.'

'Wouldn't miss it! Though Beatrice is far less fun than the normal director, who has rudely moved to Scotland.' Clio had one final spoonful of Nutella before throwing the jar back into her bag. As she did so the door swung open and in strode Beatrice herself. Short grey hair, perfect posture, thick black glasses, bright red lips. She looked like an angry ballet teacher, her head held high, nostrils flaring, eyes scanning the room, seeking her first victim. Clio saw her balling a piece of pink paper in her hands and throwing it beneath the seats as she entered. A chill wind seemed to follow her as she proceeded towards the stage, where Dexter was writing lines on his hands.

'Now, Dexter, none of that, please. I know that you can do this.' Beatrice tapped long red nails against the sweep of her black satin skirt. Her beady eyes missed nothing. 'Let's take it again from the top.'

Clio checked the time and sighed. She was meant to be attending a wreath-making workshop in Portsmouth at 6 p.m. as part of her undercover work for the Bad Girls Detective Agency, which was owned by Amber. Clio was meant to be there to establish whether the wreath-making teacher was having an affair with one of the attendees, and was in truth looking forward to an evening away from rehearsals and arguments and a lead actor who appeared to be struggling to remember his own name.

'I don't think I'm ready, Beatrice.' Clio could see how much Dexter's hands were shaking as he tried to undo his bottle of water. His voice rose higher. 'I think it's time to call this off, to – to get an understudy or something. I don't want to do this any more. I'm not ready.' His forehead was beaded with sweat and his multiple chins wobbled as he spoke. Clio found herself wondering yet again what on earth the young and beautiful Kylie saw in him. Fame, she supposed. A ticket to somewhere that wasn't here. Here she was now, coming through the back door, twirling a glossy dark curl in one of her long fingers, gazing at him adoringly. Kylie must draw attention wherever she went, yet somehow, she was dating a washed-up star whose belly was straining against his blue frock coat and who had missed one cheek when applying his fake tan. Earlier Clio had passed his dressing room and seen how white his knuckles were as they gripped his phone, as he muttered something about how he just needed more time.

'Nonsense.' Beatrice shook her head. 'Don't be so pathetic, Dexter. Start by standing up properly. Like this.' In a moment she had changed her posture, growing taller, more regal, the smile on her face so full of charm that she could be on the balcony at Buckingham Palace, waving to the crowds. 'See?' Her face sank back into its usual scowl.

Dexter reddened. 'I'm not pathetic. I'm just not ready.'

'I second that.' Ross totally failed to keep his voice down.

Clio wondered if she was ever going to get onstage. She had been out on surveillance last night, covering for Jeanie, whose twins were already on to their third vomiting bug of the festive season. Amber had been unable to help as she had been staking out a client over in Portsmouth. Since their success catching two murderers at a local luxury hotel back in February – a hotel now owned by Melissa – the agency's caseload had tripled. The three of them rarely saw each other and Clio couldn't wait to see her friends at opening night tomorrow. Then chips from the Codfather, and margaritas in Clio's static caravan up on the cliffs. Add in some karaoke carols and she would be right in the Christmas spirit. Bring it on.

She looked back at the stage. Dexter was now in full-scale meltdown, pacing up and down, his hand thrown over his eyes, every sinew of him exuding panic. 'I just can't go on…' he wailed. 'Don't make me go on, Beatrice. It's too much.'

Clio wondered if he had been on the gin again. She had heard his man bag clinking as he had left the theatre yesterday for some local press interviews, and had a funny feeling it hadn't been soft drinks in there.

Beatrice was striding up on stage, hands on hips, head level. Her mellifluous tones could be heard at the back of the auditorium, despite the hammering coming from Gawain, the set builder who was finishing up the kitchen set for the custard pie scene. Beatrice was old school – she really knew how to project. 'Dexter. You've got to stop this silly wailing and get on with it. Bite the bullet. Take that leap. Have faith.' Her thick gold rings glinted under the stage lights.

'I'm not sure anyone's allowed to call a mental breakdown "wailing" any more, are they, Ross?' Clio contemplated an unprecedented fourth helping of Nutella. She checked inside her bag for her wallet. Credit cards and phones were disappearing at alarming rates backstage, and Clio couldn't afford to lose hers. She exhaled. Both items were still there.

'Beatrice Butler doesn't care about being woke.' Ross sipped from his camomile tea. 'God, this stuff is disgusting.' He eyed Clio's tea. 'Can I…? Please, darling?'

'NO.' She frowned. 'I don't share food. Or drink. Not unless your name is

Amber or Jeanie, anyway.' She took a quick selfie and sent it to their WhatsApp chat, with a caption saying 'Next stop, Broadway.'

Quick as a flash, Amber replied. 'Ealing Broadway?'

Clio tapped back. 'If I'm lucky.'

'Shame. I could do with a decent cuppa.' Ross sat back in his seat, hands folded over his Dame Trot undergarments, which were turquoise and cumbersome, to say the least. 'Do you think Jaxon and Sylvia are actually going to kill each other inside that costume?'

'Possibly.' Clio watched Daisy the Cow, her head on one side. 'I still can't believe Beatrice put them in there together.'

'Why? She's a sadist. Always has been.' Ross shook his head. He leant towards Clio, his head angled confidentially. He loved a chat. It wasn't surprising that – outside his festive theatrical endeavours – he earnt his living selling properties. He probably talked everyone into submission until they bought a house just to get the hell out of the room.

Dexter had now passed tears and was moving swiftly towards anger. 'I am not wailing, Beatrice, I am expressing my feelings.' He stormed to the other side of the stage. 'And my feelings are that...'

Beatrice took a step towards him. Then another. But no one ever got to hear what his feelings were, nor what Beatrice thought about them. Because, as he finished speaking, something fell down from the ceiling and crashed to the ground, landing precisely on Beatrice's desk in the middle of the auditorium.

There was a very loud silence. The entire cast froze, staring at the spot where the light had landed. If Beatrice Butler had not followed Dexter onstage, then she would have been underneath that light.

'Oh my God.' Clio put her hand to her mouth. 'She could have been killed!'

'Oh my God. They missed!' Ross's hand flew to his mouth. 'Oops, did I say that out loud?'

'Ross!' Clio batted at him with her hand, trying not to laugh. 'Ssssssh.'

'Sorry.' She saw that his face was pale. 'I always joke when I'm upset.' He reached out and held her hand. His fingers were shaking and Clio held on tight. But at the same time, she was looking around the auditorium, seeing who was in here and who was missing. Because lights don't just fall down like that. Not normally. Not in any of the productions that Clio had worked on over the years.

So that begged the question: had someone deliberately dropped it? Loosened it? Wanted it to fall on Beatrice?

And if so, who had that person been?

Melissa leant forwards and spoke again. 'Is that part of panto too? Jeopardy? Peril? I like it!'

Clio shook her head.

'No. That – that was a surprise. That was... serious.'

Melissa gave a low whistle. 'Man. You three bad girls really shouldn't go anywhere, should you? Wherever you go, murder follows.'

Clio stayed silent. Melissa had a point, and Clio found herself wondering what other danger might be around the corner.

Sunshine Sands Amateur Dramatic Society
Full Cast List for "Jack and the Beanstalk"

Lead Roles
Jack: Kylie Silver
Dame Trot: Ross Jones
Fairy Moonshine, the good fairy: Dame Beatrice Butler
Daisy, Dame Trot's cow: Jaxon King and Sylvia Mae
Prince Charming: Dexter Buchanan
Blunderbore, the giant: Marg Redfearn (voice only)
Blackheart, Blunderbore's henchman: Clio Lawrence
Dancers/Chorus/Jumping Beans: Assorted members of the Sunshine Sands Sizzlers

Signed:

Dame Beatrice Butler, 15 September 2025

3
CLIO

'Oh my God, Dexter, are you okay?' Kylie was running towards the stage, her long, dark hair flying.

Beatrice looked at Kylie, coolly. 'It was nowhere near him.'

Kylie's silver bangles jangled as she threw her arms around Dexter. 'Baby. Are you okay, baby?'

Beatrice rolled her eyes, apparently more perturbed by Kylie's display of affection than she had been about the light landing on her desk.

'I'm here. Don't worry.' Kylie frowned – or tried to. Despite being only twenty, she was already a Botox aficionado, as she had told Clio excitedly on the first day of rehearsals. She had experimented with fillers too, she said, before suggesting that Clio should go and see her provider, because 'she does old ladies too, yeah?' Strangely enough, from that point onwards Clio had struggled to warm to Kylie, no matter how many times the latter offered to help her update her image 'because skinny jeans are so over, aren't they?'

Onstage, Clio saw that Daisy the Cow was gyrating frantically. At the front end, Sylvia was screaming, 'What the hell was that?' while Jaxon at the back yelled, 'Where's the Velcro? I've got to get out of this thing!' Then a loud ripping sound filled the theatre and Daisy's synthetic skin came apart in the middle.

'What happened?' Jaxon and Sylvia's heads appeared, their flushed faces taking in the smashed stage light – its weight, its position and the way it had snapped the director's desk in half.

Ever a cool character, Beatrice turned to the cast, not missing a beat, her delivery deadpan. 'So, speak up. Which one of you wants to kill me?'

This was met with an awkward smattering of laughter. Clio knew she was not alone in having fantasised about murdering Beatrice. As an actress, Beatrice liked to grab the spotlight on every occasion possible, while as a director she was a tyrant. The way she would suddenly grab an actor's script and expect them to have memorised all their lines in the very first rehearsal; the way she would openly yawn when an actor was giving it their all; the way that every single female in the cast had a costume that brought out the worst in them, while Beatrice, as Fairy Moonshine, got to parade her still-enviable figure around in a sequinned white silk gown.

After weeks of being told she was less talented than the Bic biro Beatrice used to make notes on her script, Clio had been proud of herself for staying strong, for not giving Beatrice the reaction she so clearly wanted. But then Clio had seen her costume. She had envisaged skintight black leather for her baddie role – what she got instead was a brown sack, with holes cut out for her arms, heavy black boots, green skin paint and a ginger pageboy wig. She might as well not have bothered trying to get in shape for the production – no one would be able to see her body underneath all the hessian. She had cried when she had seen herself in the mirror – she looked like a radioactive Joan of Arc.

'GAWAIN.' Beatrice's voice would put out a roaring fire. 'WHERE ARE YOU?'

The set designer ran out onto the stage, chest heaving, sweat pouring down his face. He looked down at the smashed light, his mouth working frantically.

'Oh my God.' Gawain's face drained of all colour, unlike his mustard-coloured cable-knit jumper which was maintaining its usual fluorescent glow. His thinning brown hair clung to his gleaming scalp and his tired red eyes were trained on the shattered light.

Beatrice enunciated each word in her low, smoky voice, her diction so clear that Clio could hear each syllable right at the back of the theatre. 'Gawain, whatever you did to the lights, kindly go and check the rest of them before one of us is killed. Oh, and clear the mess up too.'

Gawain looked at the mass of glass and metal, his eyes bulging. Even his hair seemed to be sweating now. 'What...?' His chest started to heave. 'Who?' He turned his face up to the ceiling above the auditorium, examining the rows of lights suspended from the long lighting bars attached to the ceiling, far above the stage and auditorium.

Gawain finally got his words out. 'What happened?'

Beatrice's voice was icy. 'Oh. Nothing much. A stage light just fell onto my desk. Luckily, I wasn't there at the time. If I had been, our incompetent set designer would have just made the biggest mistake of his life, one that might have led to a lifetime behind bars.'

Gawain had only just begun to stutter apologies when Beatrice stalked offstage, presumably to help herself to a large glass of the Campari that she always kept in her office-cum-dressing-room backstage. As a veteran of three murder hunts now, the first being to find the killer of her own ex, Gary, Clio found herself starting to wonder who could have deliberately tampered with the light. There were so many reasons to hate Beatrice Butler. She watched Dexter Buchanan, as he stood being comforted by Kylie in the corner. He was running a hand over his greying stubble, his eyes darting up towards the ceiling every few seconds. He kept moving from foot to foot, and each time he did, the buttons of his blue frock coat strained a little more.

Clio watched him. Maybe Dexter had it in for Beatrice, maybe he hated her, maybe she had forced him to be in this production somehow. Ross had told Clio on one of their many gossipy post-rehearsal drinks at The Ovation, an old-school pub just by the theatre, that he had heard the two of them having a stand-up row only the week before. Ross had been hazy on details, but said he was sure that something had been smashed. Clio wasn't entirely sure she could trust his take on things, seeing as he had once told her that he had gone on a date with Rylan, only to subsequently let slip that said date was, in fact, an appearance in the crowd on *Supermarket Sweep*.

Jaxon shrugged off the rest of the cow costume and marched down the steps. 'House lights up.' He put his hand over his eyes, to stop himself being blinded. 'I guess I'm in charge now, then?' He glared at the edge of the stage, where Beatrice had disappeared. 'Again. Not that my programme credit will even faintly reflect how much work I've put into this.'

Sylvia puffed her long blonde hair out of her eyes. 'Quit moaning, Jaxon. You wanted to be assistant director, so get on with it and direct. Okay? No one wants to hear you banging on about how hard your life is.' Clio noticed the way she was gazing at the light, her lips curving downwards as if she was disappointed. Could Sylvia somehow have set this up? She was all floaty dresses and patchouli on the surface, but maybe she had climbed up to the lighting rig when no one was around, unscrewed the light and hoped it would crush Beatrice.

Clio was distracted from her thoughts by Dexter, who had recovered himself and almost appeared invigorated by all the drama. As Jaxon started the rehearsal again, while Gawain laboriously cleared up the glass, Dexter somehow managed to remember his first line, and the next one, and even the one after that.

Ross finished typing a text and leant over to Clio, his pallor gone. 'Maybe Beatrice set up that light herself, to shock Dexter into working out how to act.'

'Maybe.' Clio nodded. For the rest of the dress rehearsal, Dexter managed not only to deliver his lines correctly, but even to occasionally remember where he was meant to be standing. For once, he didn't upstage her during her 'I'm evil but I still love Santa' dance routine, and even Ross was almost happy when Dexter remembered to bring on the custard pie to be slammed into his face later.

Beatrice returned after about half an hour and showed no evidence of enjoying any element of anyone's performance, preferring to stalk around the auditorium screaming instructions to the terrified Sizzlers, or picking on Gawain, who looked so upset that Clio even offered him some Nutella.

'I'm so sorry, Beatrice.' Gawain staggered across the stage carrying a fake rock that looked heavy enough to have been recently extracted from a quarry. 'I will try harder, I promise.'

'You may try harder, Gawain...' Beatrice examined her long red fingernails. 'But I fear it won't make any difference whatsoever.'

Gawain's eyes widened, a puppy gazing through a car window at a departing human, before he reddened and turned away. Clio thought she saw his jaw stiffen and his eyes harden. Clio had always thought he was the ultimate wet blanket, but maybe there was a backbone in there if you looked hard enough. She caught his eye and smiled, and he did his best to grin back, giving her an awkward thumbs up.

Clio waited for her big scene, her baddie tap dance over the slippery remains of the pies. She was going to give it her all, to enjoy her moment in the spotlight. When she had auditioned, she had been seeking distraction, an escape from the caravan park she called home. Set on top of the cliffs, with a panoramic view of the rusting oil tankers in the bay, it was owned by her ex,

Bez, father to Nina, Clio's daughter. Clio and Bez got along well on the whole, but recently he had found a new girlfriend, with the unlikely name of Tiara, who was at least a foot taller than Clio (not difficult, as Clio's friends liked to point out), and who was also some kind of opera singer, or so she claimed. She loved ruining Clio's mornings by launching into Wagner at 8 a.m. and had an annoying habit of running around the caravan site in her underwear while her clothes rumbled around in the communal tumble dryers. Apparently, winter only made the experience more joyful – or bracing, as Tiara said. No matter how many times her friends asked, Clio really didn't mind the fact that Bez had found love – she just minded that said love was so antisocially loud.

Her thoughts were interrupted by the production's stage manager, Winnie, an earnest brunette who was never seen moving at less than a sprint. She approached Beatrice at a steady 20 mph and tapped her on the sleeve.

Beatrice didn't even bother turning. 'Not now, Winifred.'

'But...' The girl was barely audible. The month-long rehearsal period seemed to have shrunk her in every sense of the word. At the beginning, she had still had the ability to smile, or even to laugh, when someone made a particularly amusing joke. But now she was a husk, a ghost in a tracksuit and Uggs, her long, dark hair greasy, her fringe unkempt. 'There's someone who needs to...'

Beatrice flapped her hand as if to shoo her away. It was almost as if she wanted everyone to hate her. 'I said not now. Are you deaf, girl?'

Winnie, who was nearing thirty, flushed pillar-box red.

'No, but...'

'I. Am. In. Rehearsal.' Beatrice flung a hand out theatrically. 'The muse cannot be interrupted. I will not stand for it. Go. Away.'

'It's just that...' Winnie hovered, a fly about to smash into a windscreen. 'Um.'

'Um?' Beatrice's voice was rising. 'You come to me with "UM"?'

'You asked me to tell you, when...'

Beatrice swung round, a cat about to pounce.

'Sorry.' Winnie threw the words over her shoulder while running out of the room, her arms over her head as if she was trying to protect herself in a hurricane.

Beatrice inhaled slowly through her long nostrils. 'Now then.' She looked around the room. 'Everyone just remember, we must concentrate, we must...'

She arched her eyebrows impatiently. 'Focus, everyone. What have I been saying all these weeks?'

'We must do as Beatrice says.' The cast droned this with all the excitement of members of a chain gang hearing a whip being cracked. As they finished, Daisy the Cow toppled over sideways, leading to the rip in the costume reopening, and to yet more arguing from Jaxon and Sylvia. Beatrice looked at her watch meaningfully as the two of them bickered.

'I told you we were stepping forward.' Sylvia's voice would shatter glass. 'You never bloody listen!'

Jaxon wiped his glasses on the black and white fur. 'You're a fine one to talk. You never listen either. If you did, then you wouldn't have gone and...'

'You two. Stop it now.' Beatrice's eyes glinted.

Sylvia was taking no prisoners. 'You can't talk to me like that, Beatrice. I told you not to put us together. I begged you to keep us apart. But oh no, you had to—'

'Be quiet.' There was no arguing with Beatrice's tone. She clapped her hands together. 'Now, we will take a short break, while...'

A loud whisper from Ross. 'While Beatrice goes and has some gin. And while I try to pretend that Dexter is in any way ready to play this part.'

Clio stifled a giggle. Jaxon twirled his cow's tail while Beatrice glared at Ross with such hatred that Clio was quite surprised he didn't fall to the ground.

She stalked past them. 'No one wants to hear what you think, Ross. So kindly keep your opinions to yourself.'

'Love you too.' Ross yawned so openly that Clio wondered if he had some kind of death wish. 'I don't know why we all put up with her,' he mused.

Clio exhaled and sat down on the stage, casting a nervous glance up at the lights, just in case. 'Because she's a theatrical legend.'

'No. Because this is her last show and we love the attention.' Ross smiled. 'It's going to be rammed to the rafters with her fans coming out to see her one last time.'

'Why doesn't she seem more happy about it then?' Melissa appeared again, back from taking pictures of the Jumping Beans. 'She looks miserable.'

Ross nodded knowingly. 'She doesn't want the theatre to close. Can't accept it. Even though the writing is all over the bloody wall, now, isn't it? She'd kill to keep it open, I reckon.'

'Well, we wouldn't want that, would we?' Clio stuck another spoon of sugar into her tea and stirred. 'I'm trying to steer clear of murder for a while.'

She sipped the sweet liquid, seeing that was already 5 p.m., knowing that they still had the big finale to rehearse. She wondered if she should make the call and text Amber saying she was going to be late for wreath-making. Or maybe Melissa could cover her?

Yes. Some time off murders was just what she needed. It was nearly Christmas so it was time for unrealistic to-do lists, failing to buy wrapping paper, eating her own bodyweight in Christmas cake, singing carols at every opportunity, pantomime applause and then Christmas dinner with Bez and their daughter Nina, hopefully minus Tiara and her trilling. That was what Clio wanted for Christmas. Nothing more. Nothing less. Stanley Tucci turning up to cook her an Italian feast would be acceptable too, but Clio knew not to be too picky.

Looking up, she saw Kylie stalking after Beatrice, her mouth set, waving a piece of paper in her hand.

Clio felt a spark of curiosity and then told herself not to be silly. She went back to her tea. It was probably nothing.

No one would want to kill anyone over a panto, would they?

ONE DAY LATER

OPENING NIGHT

4

JEANIE

Jeanie stood in the theatre foyer, already regretting her decision to wear her Christmas jumper to her only night out in the past month. Sweat was prickling under her armpits, and it seemed that the shop's website had been optimistic in its claim that the jumper would be soft and sensual against her skin. *Resembles barbed wire* might have been a more accurate description, thought Jeanie, as her HRT patch utterly failed to contain the fires within her.

There was still nearly an hour to go until curtain up, but a few fellow show-goers were as early as her. They were busy stamping snow off their shoes and shrugging off coats that were starting to steam, before beginning the important task of getting the drinks in at the bar. Jeanie smiled to herself, grateful to be out of the house at last. Her nearly three-year-old twins were finally free to roam, following a demoralising few weeks as they passed the pre-school sickness baton – and sick buckets – back and forth. But Jeanie had been determined to get them to the show tonight – determined that they see their godmum Clio in her element onstage, and excited about sharing their first ever Christmas pantomime with them.

She looked down, feeling a sudden desire to hug them, only for her heart to miss a beat. They weren't there. They had been right next to her only a matter of seconds ago, and yet already Yumi and Jack had found a way to disappear. Jeanie scanned the room, but could see no thick black hair, no huge brown eyes, no matching red puffa coats adorned with silver tinsel since the Sunshine Sands Christmas Fair last Saturday.

'Oh no. Not again.' Jeanie turned her head frantically, trying to see Yumi's reindeer antlers or Jack's Santa hat, only to realise that there were several other small children present, also sporting festive headgear. Of course there were – this was the only Christmas panto in town. Jeanie berated herself for at least the twentieth time that day as she continued to search for her children. She was getting so good at telling herself off that she might start listing it on her CV. She should have dressed them in something distinctive, like hard hats or those ludicrous luminous yellow snoods that Takako, her mother-in-law, had sent them from Tokyo for their birthdays. Anything would have been better than what Jeanie had chosen.

Heat started to spiral inside her and she tried to pull the neck of her jumper away from her skin to create some kind of cooling mechanism. Her twins could be anywhere by now, with so many doors and passageways to choose from, and if they had one reliable characteristic, it was their tendency to head in opposite directions. Their other habit was, if anything, more problematic and she hoped that when she found them, they wouldn't be secreting any stolen items in their pockets or under their jumpers. In the past month alone Jeanie had been reprimanded at least weekly by their childminder Noleen for their light-fingered ways, aided by the fact that they had developed their own language to plan their misdeeds. Nothing could ever take away the sting of having to apologise to Noleen for Jack escaping into the utility room at her house and scribbling all over every single item in her white wash with a scarlet lipstick that Yumi had stolen from her pocket.

Jeanie flushed at the memory, even as she started to move through the foyer in search of her children. People were chatting and laughing, enjoying the lovely evening out that Jeanie had hoped for. She called her children's names as she moved, even though it would be highly unusual for them to be listening out for her voice.

A door opened to her left and Jeanie heard her name. She whirled around to see her best friend, Clio, beckoning her across. Jeanie walked towards her, feeling a surge of relief as she entered a dark passageway and saw that her friend was clutching Yumi in one hand and Jack in the other. The twins, for once, were silent, probably intimidated by Clio's fierce stage make-up, which made her look like a particularly hungover version of the Grinch. Clio's chin-length bob, recently bleached blonde, had been gelled back and covered with an unflattering red wig in the shape of Jeanie's childhood pudding bowl haircut. Meanwhile, her skin had been painted the greenish hue of the mould that remained an unwelcome visitor in Jeanie's bathroom, no matter how much Dettol she threw at it.

Clio arched an eyebrow. 'I found these two scurrying around by the props cupboard. I thought you might want them back, Jeanie? Beatrice doesn't like anyone being back here who isn't involved in the show, so...'

'Of course! Thanks for catching them for me, Clio. And I'm so sorry.' Jeanie took her children by the hand, hanging on tight as they predictably started to squirm. She turned for the door, reflecting that, after years of IVF, absolutely nothing about motherhood was the way she expected it to be. She had sleep-walked her way through the first year, wielding bottles and purees and nappies in a never-ending cycle, anticipating that everything would get easier when the twins grew older. Instead, she now found herself looking back on the baby years with the kind of nostalgia she had previously reserved for pictures of herself in her twenties – so unwrinkled, so uncreased, so wide-eyed. When they were babies, they hadn't been able to move. If only Jeanie had appreciated what a bonus that was.

She eyed Clio, weighing her words carefully. 'Um. You look...?'

'Hideous?' Clio was never one to understate things. Ever since Jeanie, Clio and Amber had met while not being picked for PE at school, Clio had always brought the drama to their trio. Nothing was a minor event with Clio – she was a one-woman miniseries, her life a succession of bad dates and big dreams.

Clio scowled, gesturing to her costume, speaking in a whisper. 'Bloody Beatrice. This is all her fault. She told me when I got the part that I was going to be the glamorous villainess, but instead I look like I've recently been harvested from a toxic compost heap. This costume is a literal sack.' She indicated the brown hessian disdainfully. 'And I swear I am coming out in some kind of rash. Look at this!' She pointed to a tiny red mark on her hand. 'See? It might be hives!'

'It's not hives, Clio.' Jeanie bent down, trying to keep hold of Jack, who was disturbingly strong for someone who only came up to her knees. She wondered if today was the day that her back was finally going to give up the struggle, after nearly three years of leaning over at half-mast in a vain attempt to keep her children under control.

Jack pulled harder. 'Mama goooooooo.'

'No, Jack.' Jeanie tipped her neck upwards, trying to maintain some kind of semblance of adult conversation. 'You look great, Clio. Seriously. Very evil.'

Clio raised her eyebrows. 'And you, Jeanie, are the world's worst liar.' She shook her head. 'But you are very kind to try. This situation—' she gestured to her hessian apparel '—is beyond compliments, I think. Beyond everything, really.' She knelt so she was on a level with Yumi, who instantly started crying, turning in to cling on to Jeanie's leg. 'See?' She raised her eyes to Jeanie.

'I'm so sorry.' Jeanie made some cooing sounds, which had absolutely no effect whatsoever. 'Beatrice is going to freak out, isn't she?'

'Her dressing room is right down the end through some double doors, so she probably won't hear it.' Clio shrugged. 'She banished the dancers to the cafe across the square, and took over their studio as her dressing room. It's huge, naturally – it's down that corridor there.' She pointed to the one branching left, ahead of them. 'While I have Ross King next to me, who is currently talking so loudly on his phone that I came out here for some peace and met these two scamps.'

'Sorry.' Jeanie cringed. 'But I'm glad you did.'

Clio lifted her right foot up as Jack made another heroic attempt at escape. Jeanie's fingers were starting to ache. 'I mean, how am I meant to dance if I'm worried about tripping over my own feet in these mad boots?' She jabbed a finger downward to what looked like steel-toecap DMs. 'They weigh a ton. My sacrum is all off beam. My yoga teacher will kill me.'

'Um. Yes. That's really tough.' Jeanie was aware of a woman with long, dark hair and a blunt fringe who sprinted through from the Beatrice corridor and stared at Jeanie as Jack started a low-level (for him) scream. 'Stop it, Jack.' She tried her most ingratiating tone. 'Why don't we go back to the foyer and get a snack?' This idea was not met with the enthusiasm she was hoping for. Jack moved on to stage two of proceedings, starting to do his favourite escapologist full body twist, and Yumi looked horribly like she was about to start screaming too. 'But I'm sure you'll pull it off, Clio. You always do.' She did her best to muster an encouraging smile while her body was relentlessly pulled in two different directions.

'Yes!' Clio's words cut effortlessly through the chattering crowd. She hadn't been to drama school for nothing. 'I know I do, but Beatrice really has gone too far this time. God, I could kill her, I really could. I knew she was a tigress when I joined the cast, but she told us all it was going to be fun, to be her last ever show, playing to packed houses, in tribute to her late husband, and that we were all going to have a fantastic time.' She was lost in her spiral, completely oblivious to Jeanie's wriggling children. 'But frankly, it's been like being directed by a nuclear warhead. Everyone in the cast is miserable. Jaxon made a dartboard with her face on it last night, and I scored 180.'

Jeanie lowered her voice to try to calm her friend. 'Well, all that's over now. It's opening night. Your big moment. And we can't wait to watch you up there in the spotlight.' She wondered if she might at last develop biceps from holding on to her own children. At least that would be something positive to come out of all the holding on she was doing nowadays.

'I mean, it's just weird, the whole Beatrice thing. She doesn't seem to have any friends, but she still doesn't want to spend any time with her cast.' Clio was on a roll. She had never been a woman to hold back. She had never had any filter, not even back when they were teenagers and she had told Jeanie that the dress she wanted to wear to the school disco was 'optimistic'. However, she was also one of the kindest people Jeanie had ever met, the one who made Jeanie give the final round of IVF a go, the one who checked in every single morning with an emoji or a funny llama meme – a woman who made the phrase 'friends forever' ring true.

'Beatrice has made this whole show a nightmare. I love doing amateur pantomime normally, but never again. Frankly, if I did kill Beatrice the others would applaud me. If they didn't get there first, that is.' Clio nodded decisively. She peered around the corridor, having predictably left her much-hated glasses in her dressing room. 'Where's Amber, anyway? Is she going to get here before curtain up?'

Jeanie winced as Jack started trying to prise her fingers away from his wrist, one by one. 'Don't worry, she's on her way. Her new client interview ran late, but she promises she'll be here on time. NO, JACK.' Too late. Jack had wrenched himself away and sprinted down the corridor, his little arms pumping. A wave of exhaustion overcame Jeanie, and she wondered again why motherhood never seemed to come with any form of respite. She craved five minutes to read a magazine or a book, to simply stare out of the window and look at the sun. Then she felt guilty for even wanting time to herself when she had two such beautiful children, and the cycle continued for another day and then another and suddenly she looked about seventy-five when she looked at herself in the mirror.

She called out as loudly as she dared. 'Jack. Come back. Now.'

He ignored her, of course he did. Jeanie wished she had kept a firm hold of him in the first place, distracting him with the snack stall that had been set up next to the bar in the foyer. Jeanie's tummy rumbled as she thought of the pigs in blankets, the gingerbread men and of course the mince pies. She was starving, despite having finished most of the twins' beans on toast earlier, rather than scraping the remains into the bin.

If only her husband, Tan, had been able to come to see the pantomime tonight too. After a period of enforced unemployment following a brush with the law last year, he had at last got a new job, working cash in hand at a local delivery company, and a lot of his shifts were at night. She missed him and not only because the twins were easier to manage when he was around. Between her work at the detective agency and his shifts, they had become parental baton-passers, rather than a team. Jeanie missed family outings, missed any sense that they were man and wife rather than overwhelmed parents to their increasingly unruly children. Their most romantic moments nowadays were when one of them offered to take out the bins.

'Well, I hope she makes it.' Clio sighed. 'Because my big song is ten minutes in, if Dexter manages to remember his cue and lets us get that far. He missed it earlier, so we skipped the whole thing.'

Jeanie nodded. She was more than familiar with Clio's views on Dexter Buchanan, shared via the best friends' Bad Girls WhatsApp group at every hour of the day and night. Jeanie had initially been sad to have another idol crashing to the ground. She had loved Dexter when he was on *EastEnders*, giving it his all as he punched and rebelled his way to a tumultuous marriage that ended – inevitably – in murder. Jeanie would run home with Amber and Clio to watch the episodes that Clio taped religiously on her video player, while drinking Fanta and eating Skips. To hear that in reality he was rude and prone to seducing very young women had been dispiriting, to say the least. Hearing Clio slating him reminded Jeanie of the Christmas Eve when, aged seven, she had discovered that Father Christmas did not exist. She had been curling up under the covers when her dad had bumped into her bunk bed and said, 'damn,' before delivering Jeanie's packed Christmas stocking to the end of her Strawberry Shortcake duvet.

Clio continued, having apparently forgotten that Jeanie wasn't meant to be backstage and that one of her children had absconded. 'You know, Dexter is always putting himself right at the front of the stage. He can't bear to be out of the spotlight. He's such a stage hog.'

Having been in several school shows alongside Clio, Jeanie thought this was a case of the pot calling the kettle black. Clio had once barged her out of the way during a crowd scene in *Kiss Me, Kate*, despite the fact that Jeanie had been about to say her only line at the time. Just as she was about to remind Clio of this, a thickset man rushed up to them, dressed in a greying corset that spread into a series of hoops around his bulky thighs. His brown hair was drawn back beneath a wig cap and his eyelids sported bright green eyeshadow and the longest false eyelashes Jeanie had ever seen. 'Where's Beatrice, Clio? I need to have a word.'

Clio arched an eyebrow at Jeanie. 'You remember Ross, aka our Pantomime Dame?' She turned back to the man. 'What's she done now?'

'She's only gone and cut my big song. "Man! I Feel Like a Woman!"' He huffed indignantly. 'She says I'm not ready for the key change.' He swelled to twice his actual size, his jowls flapping in indignation. 'I mean, how dare she? How many pantos have I been in now, over the years, with other, more reasonable directors? How many crowds have I wowed? I got three standing ovations last year.' He collapsed forwards, head in hands and Jeanie got a very clear view of his bald spot.

'Don't let her get you down.' Clio patted him on the shoulder. 'It's like she's trying to get us all to hate her, isn't it? What is she thinking?'

Jeanie needed to go and look for Jack, but felt the need to start comforting Ross too – she was always like this, unable to tolerate anyone else's distress, somehow feeling responsible when anyone dropped their change in the street or tripped over a loose paving stone. And, as she reached out to pat his arm, she inevitably felt another little hand leaving hers. She grabbed for it, but was too late. 'Oh no.'

She felt a pang of panic as Yumi ran after Jack. Jeanie couldn't see them, and bad things happened when she couldn't see them. 'Sorry, Clio. Break a leg, Ross!' She sprinted after her children, her body aflame, and saw once she had rounded the corner that they seemed to be heading left, down the corridor that led to Beatrice's dressing room.

'Oh no!' Jeanie squealed as the two of them cannoned through a door that said 'Actors and Production Team Only.' Jeanie saw it shut behind them, prevented from pursuit by a piece of scenery that was parked across the corridor. By the time she had circumnavigated it, the antlers and the Santa hat had disappeared through the door, leaving Jeanie absolutely no choice but to follow.

'Oh God, oh God, oh God.' The show started in half an hour – there was no way the three of them should be back here, so close to Beatrice's dressing room. Jeanie could remember her playing a terrifying Miss Havisham in a BBC Sunday night production a few years back, and shuddered. The door squeaked shut behind Jeanie and she found herself in a dark space that smelt of wood, sweat and paint. The high ceilings seemed to whisper, and she tripped over another piece of scenery as she hastened after her children. The two of them ran ahead, bubbling with all the energy they never displayed during swimming lessons, giggling, talking in their strange language, too far away for her to see them. They were absolutely definitely too close to the stage. She had to catch up with them.

A man hurried past Jeanie, heading the same way, wearing a thick cable-knit jumper, checking his watch as if worried he was about to be late for something. Jeanie ran past, accidentally bumping him with her elbow, surprised when he got his apology out first: 'So sorry.' He spoke in a deep Welsh accent. 'I'm all fingers and thumbs today.'

'No worries.' Jeanie halted as she heard raised voices coming from a room to her left, where the door, covered in silver stars, had been left standing open. It must be Beatrice's dressing room. Jeanie felt her pulse spiral. The man stopped too, and Jeanie collided with him again. 'I'm so sorry.' They spoke in unison. He smiled.

'It's fine. Really.' He hovered uncertainly, as the argument raged inside the room.

Jeanie heard a woman's voice, dripping with venom. 'I hate you, Beatrice Butler.'

She looked ahead, seeing her twins disappearing down a passageway that she had a horrible feeling might lead towards the stage. 'No! Come back!' She propelled herself forward again, leaving the man to it. Jeanie swore quietly to herself. At this rate she wouldn't be watching the show at all, she would be hunting for her lost children throughout the entire thing. She had missed an entire 'SpongeBob' movie last week for the same reason and had eventually found Yumi and Jack hiding in the staff coat cupboard, face-deep in buckets of popcorn.

As she followed the twins, the voices behind her escalated.

'You have no right to hate me.' Beatrice sounded beyond frosty. 'I have given you so much and now you are throwing it back in my face.'

'Because you promised more. And now I find out you've gone behind my back, and…'

Over her shoulder, Jeanie saw the man still lingering by dressing room door. He lifted his hand towards the handle, then dropped it again. Lifted, and dropped. Jeanie wondered if he would find the courage to go inside, or if he would still be waiting at the door as the curtain went up.

Jeanie had no choice but to hurry on, her mind full of questions. Where were Jack and Yumi? Why was she not a better mum? Why did everything go wrong? Why was her jumper so scratchy? And why did everyone in this cast hate each other so much? By the time Jeanie had reached the end of the corridor and burst through another door she was wondering whether this show really was going to go on. She saw Yumi and Jack about to pick up some custard pies from a props table in the wings.

'NO!'

Her voice was so forceful, that for once, her children were surprised into stopping what they were doing, and she scooped up the two of them, ignoring their protests as they wriggled and screamed, carrying them bodily back towards the corridor, one under each arm, using her shoulder to open the doors.

As she passed Beatrice's dressing room on the way back, she heard a different voice. A Welsh voice, this time, the man she had just seen. 'Beatrice, I'm just asking you to listen to me. Please. Just listen. Why won't you ever listen to me?'

'Why on earth would I listen to you…' A pause as Jack elbowed Jeanie in the face. Jeanie held in her response, wanting to hear what Beatrice replied. That famous rich voice continued. '…when you are just telling me lies?'

Yumi let out a squeal that nearly shattered Jeanie's eardrum and, heart pounding under the weight of the two of them, she lumbered onwards.

Five minutes later they were back in the foyer and Jeanie was breathing a heavy sigh of relief. Her arms were screaming, but she had no choice but to hold both children by the hand, and to buy a huge bag of Haribo to keep them quiet. Forget teeth. Forget dentists. Jeanie needed peace. She checked her watch. Only fifteen minutes till showtime. As Jack and Yumi chomped on the sweets, she reflected that she should probably check their pockets, to check they hadn't stolen anything. She really was living the parental dream.

The three of them entered the auditorium with seconds to spare, after two emergency visits to the loo, only to discover that they were in the middle of a long row of red velvet seats in the middle of the stalls. Jack and Yumi cannoned their way towards them, upending several glasses of wine and boxes of Christmas chocolates as they went. Many disapproving expressions and apologies later, they landed in seats 14 to 16, and Jeanie was just removing the twins' coats and scarves when she saw her friend Amber coming in to join them. Amber's short, dark hair was white with snow, and she stamped her ubiquitous trainers on the floor, mouth curving downwards in her traditional Christmas grimace.

'Ugh.' She slid into the seat next to Jeanie. 'I bloody hate Christmas.'

Jeanie checked to see that her children were distracted by the sweets she had bought them and was pleased to discover that yes, they had missed this particular word choice from the third member of her trio.

'I thought I was going to be late.' Amber looked at her phone and pointed in the direction of the thick red curtain currently obscuring the stage. 'I hope they start on time. I've got to be out on surveillance again by eleven.'

Jeanie opened her mouth to tell Amber that she was working too hard, then thought better of it and closed it again. After several decades of friendship, she had learnt that giving Amber advice never made any difference – she rarely followed anything other than her own gut instinct.

Amber nudged her. 'How hyped is Clio? Did you give her the Nutella for rehearsals? Has she downed it all in one?'

Jeanie grinned. 'I did. I saw her backstage just now. She was mainly angry to be honest. Something about her costume being disgusting and everyone wanting to kill Beatrice Butler.'

Amber nodded. 'Melissa called earlier to say she can't make it – she's covering a shift at the hotel, but she'll be here later. She said someone dropped a light on Beatrice's desk in rehearsal, or something. She's loving the drama.' She rolled her eyes, but Jeanie had a strong suspicion that Amber was enjoying having a real blood relative at last. 'Why, is Clio's costume too tight, or something?'

Jeanie giggled as she thought of the hessian sack Clio had been wearing. She never knew how much she missed her friends until she saw them again and they set the world to rights. The three of them had been so busy working recently – all on different cases in different locations – that they hadn't had the time to connect. 'The opposite. It reminded me of her peasant costume in *Les Mis*, when everyone was ill so she had to play about forty parts, including Eponine.'

Amber smiled too. 'Was that the one where the barricades collapsed while Clio was still singing?'

'Yes.' Jeanie saw that Yumi was running low on sweets and delved into her bag for the next snack. She might not have much expertise in other aspects of being a parent, but she did have a serious talent for feeding her children up. She even had some food pre-prepared in Tupperware, so that her children wouldn't emit the sound of crinkling plastic for the whole of the performance. She sat back in her seat and looked around the auditorium. Jeanie loved watching shows. All around her, people talked and murmured, waiting expectantly to see the actors take to the stage.

The Beatrice Butler Theatre smelt of mulled wine, mince pies and some indefinable greasepaint and sawdust combination that Jeanie had always thought of as the essence of theatre. She and Amber were veterans of every show Clio had ever been in – even that terrible one at the Edinburgh Festival about periods – and as such she had experienced the indefinable expectation of opening night many times. It never got old. Each time she sat in a theatre seat and waited for the show to begin, she always felt her hopes rising, a sense of optimism about what was about to unfold, the expectation of escaping into a new story.

'What are they doing back there? It should definitely have started by now.' Amber reached into her pocket and extracted a can of ready-mixed margarita.

'I don't know.' Jeanie felt a prickle of unease. Whatever her faults, Beatrice Butler was famous for running a tight ship. When she was little, Jeanie had watched Beatrice in a series called *Top Deck*, in which Beatrice's landed duchess character had an on-off affair with a bus driver called Kevin. It had been a Sunday evening highlight for Jeanie's parents, who would crack open a box of Quality Street and some sherry and put their feet up. And now, Clio was in one of her shows. Jeanie felt a quiet surge of pride for her friend. She was doing her thing: reaching for a life outside the hectic schedule of being a detective: of nights on surveillance and days tailing marks. Jeanie couldn't wait to see her friend back up on stage, where she belonged.

The spotlight appeared and someone was emerging from behind the curtains. But it wasn't the tall, graceful figure of Beatrice Butler. Instead, someone else was blinking into the limelight. A man with thick glasses and a pork-pie hat. The spotlight relentlessly picked out his shaking hands and when he spoke his voice wobbled. He was clearly a man with very bad news to share.

He pushed his thick black glasses higher up his nose. From Clio's description this must be Jaxon, the assistant director, aka the front end of the pantomime cow. He looked like he wished he was wearing his costume now.

He placed one hand against the other, rubbing his palms together.

'Ladies and gentlemen, I am so sorry to have to tell you that tonight's performance is cancelled. Something has happened that is beyond our control, and we have no other option but to cancel the show. We are incredibly sorry.'

Yumi looked up from her snack, then shrugged and started eating again as the audience gave a general groan.

Amber nudged Jeanie, her eyes bright. 'What do you think is going on back there?'

Jeanie shrugged. 'I don't know, but it can't be good, can it?'

'WHAT'S THAT?' One old lady on the end of the row was asking her partner what was happening. 'I CAN'T HEAR ANYTHING. IS HE THE GENIE?'

Her companion shushed her gently, while behind Jeanie a mobile phone went off. Jaxon raised both hands as if to placate the sold-out audience. 'Please forgive us, but we have to cancel the performance because...' He searched for words, even wiping a tear from his cheek. 'Because our director, Beatrice Butler...' He visibly gathered himself, pulling himself up to his full height. He gave a sweeping gesture with his hands, as if to take them all along with him.

'Because our esteemed director, Beatrice Butler, is dead.'

5

BEATRICE BUTLER

08.25: Eleven hours until her death

On the morning of her death, Beatrice Butler woke up with every intention of making the most of every minute of her day. She lay there in the four-poster bed she had shared with her husband, Florian, until his death five years ago, enjoying the smooth silk sheets against her skin. Today was the day. Today she would secure the future of the Beatrice Butler Theatre for ever and her name would become immortal. No matter what anyone said, she was going to do things her way, to take control, to forge the future she wanted. She might be seventy-five, but she was far from a feeble old woman. Whatever people thought, she was still a force to be reckoned with.

She levered herself up, leaning back against her formidable bank of goose feather pillows, and reached out a hand to swing her breakfast tray across in front of her. Her Italian housekeeper, Magda, was back to her impressive best, after a small bout of unreliability during a dalliance with a Polish window cleaner. Realising that her trusty servant was about to leave, Beatrice had rapidly seen him off with two thousand pounds and vague threats about immigration law. She felt no guilt about this whatsoever – in fact, she felt that she had done Magda a favour in getting rid of the man. Nobody whose eyes are that close together could ever really be trusted; Magda really should understand that at her age.

Beatrice looked down at the golden tray in satisfaction. Magda set it silently by her bed every morning just before Beatrice's 'Golden Flute' alarm clock, a gift from darling Alec Guinness, went off. Beatrice sighed happily as she surveyed the tray. There it all was, just as it had always been, the breakfast she and Florian had eaten every day since they had married in the early 1980s: Assam tea steaming in a small Japanese pot that he had bought her for her fortieth birthday; the bright pink cup that Sir Ian McKellen had given her when they had starred in *Much Ado about Nothing* together; her morning toast cut into the dainty triangles that Beatrice preferred.

Beatrice poured her tea into the cup, adding a slice of lemon, and taking her first sip. Fortified, she reached for the thick black notebook that was always beside her bed. She picked up her heavy black fountain pen, forcing her shaking fingers into submission, and began to write on the thick cream paper, a small smile on her face. She wrote her diary every single day, chronicling whatever had happened during the previous twenty-four hours in her looping writing.

She knew that when she was gone the world would be hungry for these memories, and sometimes, she had to admit, she might exaggerate a story or two, just for dramatic effect. As such, the day it was published might be a difficult one for certain people who had worked with her, or who had dared to block her path. Back when she was mere Betty White, the popcorn girl at her local cinema, she had known that she would face her fair share of obstacles in getting to the top. Now, she was extracting her revenge on paper, one word at a time, and she always felt somehow replenished once she had screwed the cap back on her pen and set the diary to one side.

As she described the meeting she had arranged yesterday, and her excitement about where it might lead, she felt determination rising inside her. She was really going to pull it off this time. No more relying on others – she was doing it all herself, just as Florian had expected of her. He had asked so little of her, really, in all their years together. He had always put her first, let her light shine. Now it was time for Beatrice to repay him.

She started on her toast, taking the small, delicate bites of a woman who had spent years controlling her calorie intake and reached for her other morning staple – her cuttings book. Today she was returning to the early 2000s, aka the years in which she had played a lot of matriarchs. Great mothers, failing mothers, aspiring mothers – she had become them all. She spent some time drinking her tea and turning over the thick white pages, admiring the way that she was now on to her fifteenth leather-bound album, spanning her fifty-year career. Yesterday morning she had relived the 2010s, gazing at pictures of her glorious Cleopatra at the National Theatre, or her Lady Bracknell at the Savoy. Judi Dench had loved that one, cackling away in the front row as Beatrice did the handbag speech. Beatrice still wasn't entirely sure how Judi had landed a damehood ahead of her, but had always suspected foul play. No one who seemed that nice was ever actually that nice. It stood to reason, didn't it?

She spotted a note from Magda resting on the side of the tray and sighed. She hoped it wasn't more nonsense about going on holiday next month. How could the woman possibly prefer some filthy hotel room overlooking some Italian bins to remaining here in Beatrice's spacious seafront Georgian apartment? How misguided people were. Last year Magda had even dared to ask for a pay rise, talking about inflation, about some kind of cost-of-living crisis, seemingly unaware of how outrageous it was to want to extract more money from a lady of Beatrice's age. Beatrice had kept calm and allowed her to keep her job, despite this flagrant attempt at blackmail. Beatrice was too kind for her own good, her husband Florian had always said so. He had always been able to see the best in her.

The note mentioned a man coming to see Beatrice yesterday, someone who didn't want to leave his name. Beatrice raised an eyebrow. She knew exactly who it must have been. She crumpled it up, dismissing the irritation that prickled along her spine. Then, her walk down memory lane complete, she began her vocal warm-ups for the day. She did scales to start with, beginning on middle C and rising upwards, then on to diction, with plosive 'p's and clear 'k's. Once she was finished, she was ready to get out of bed. She felt unusually excited at the prospect, especially given how challenging the last few months had been. She was ready to stir the pot, to set cats amongst pigeons, to raise the tempers of the people in her cast. Tonight was opening night and she was going to make sure that it was one to remember.

Beatrice pushed the tray away, sat up straight and slid her feet into her ballet slippers. Then she walked across the thick carpet and stood by the huge sash window that overlooked the sea. There, she began her warm-up stretches, movements that she had completed every single day of her life since she had turned twenty-one. As her arms rose high above her head, she reflected that she really had assembled the perfect cast for her final production. Not because they were setting the stage alight – frankly she had seen more energy in a squashed banana than this lot brought to the tale of *Jack and the Beanstalk*. Beatrice, despite her advanced age, had more energy than the whole bunch put together. And they took offence so easily! Beatrice had heard talk of snowflakes and millennials, but in her experience midlife males were the real moaners. Dexter had begged her to cast him, playing on their old TV relationship as mother and son, back in the day. He thought he was going to get his big comeback after what could politely be termed a fallow patch, but he was going to get a whole lot more than that. Beatrice knew all his little secrets and she intended to use them to her advantage.

Beatrice began her t'ai chi swings, swaying back and forth, feeling her body beginning to wake up. Today she would also deal with Jaxon. He just needed a little prod, a carrot dangled in front of him. When he had approached her after hearing about the production, brandishing a terrible pantomime script, she had known he was perfect for her purposes. She had rejected the script, full of banal one-liners and unexciting scenes, but had taken him on as assistant director. A few weeks of undermining him had seen him come nicely to the boil – just as she had known he would.

She stretched down now, proud to still be able to reach her toes. Jaxon had babbled on about how he had once written three episodes of *Holby City*, but Beatrice soon shut him up by telling him that he had been cast as the back end of the pantomime cow. She could have got a couple of the Sunshine Sizzlers to do it, but frankly it was far more fun seeing the rage on his face. She had enjoyed the way it had disappeared as he realised that the front end of the cow would be Sylvia Mae, the stunning blonde costume designer who thought Beatrice could help her get to Hollywood.

The two of them hit it off, disappearing outside for smoke breaks and going to the pub together religiously after rehearsals. But Beatrice wasn't interested in equilibrium and calm, and so she had lobbed in a grenade, putting the two of them at each other's throats. Today, they were going to learn what she had done, and Beatrice was ready for whatever came next. They would play right into her hands.

She had one plan today and she wasn't going to be deflected. She was going to go to the meeting she had arranged and get her own way. Talking until everyone else had given up was her preferred strategy, one she had employed a thousand times in various discordant productions over the years. But there was another way, she knew. A backup. An insurance policy. Now sitting at her beautiful white dressing table, complete with an oval spot-lit mirror, she set her short grey hair into its customary style, the fringe swept back off her face. She then applied her make-up exactly the same way as she had for the last fifty years, enlarging her almond eyes with eyeliner, enhancing her cheekbones and finally brushing her face with setting powder before applying her signature blood-red lipstick. Then she took a small silver key from the china dish on her dressing table, next to the heavy hairbrush and her talcum powder.

She carried the key across to a small lacquered chest of drawers, black with a gold leaf design, and inserted it into the lock. There was a small click, and the drawer opened. Beatrice smiled as she saw the contents. One of Florian's most precious gifts. For years this object had lain in here, waiting for her. She had known it was there, an insurance policy, but she had never expected she would need to use it.

But today, someone was going to be picking this up – the only question was who. Yesterday, she had sat there in her dressing room, staring at the cast and crew pictures on her wall, and wondering which one of them it would be. She was a Dame, she had dined with the Queen, she was the face of a dementia charity, she even had Sir David Attenborough's phone number – yet even a woman with all Beatrice's life experiences could have no idea which one of them would take the bait.

All she knew was that she was running out of time. And someone knew her secret, a secret she had spent her entire life covering up so completely that no one would ever find out what it was. It had been the right thing to do, of course. She had never had any doubts about that. As she had held her BAFTA lifetime achievement award high above her head in 2018 she had thought of the moment that her life had divided into the before and the after. She had looked into the bright lights, staring out at all those famous faces, feeling a swell of satisfaction about everything she had done. There was no way she would let the truth come out now. No way on earth.

She reached out a hand and stroked the metal object with the tip of her finger. It was silver, small and elegantly wrought. She felt a thrill of danger as she looked down at it. Then she picked up the small pistol, slid it into her handbag, and let herself out of the apartment with her head held high.

As she walked down the wide steps to the lobby she nodded a hello to Carl, the concierge.

'Good morning, Dame Beatrice.'

'It is, isn't it?' She favoured him with a smile. 'It's going to be a wonderful day.'

He held open the heavy front door for her and she emerged, slipping on the Chanel sunglasses she had owned for the past twenty years. She could hear seagulls crying above her, the beep of the pedestrian crossing on the corner, a child protesting that he wanted sweets for breakfast. She shuddered at his high-pitched whine.

She was so grateful she had never become a mother. There had been no room in her and Florian's relationship for anyone else, no room for a third wheel in their happy coexistence. She had loved him ever since they had turned up to that terrible pub theatre, which smelt of wee and disinfectant, to begin *Jack and the Beanstalk* rehearsals. The turn of his head, the thick, dark hair and those blue eyes shining over his half-moon glasses. She had fallen, instantly, as had he, and within a week they were engaged.

It had helped that he was wealthy, of course, with an annual allowance so huge that he could fund the productions that got her started, with money left over for the kind of marketing campaign that got bums on seats. All Beatrice had to do was be the star she was born to be. He came from the kind of family who went to Balmoral for Christmas and owned multiple estates across the world. With Florian came a luxury that little Betty had only dreamt of. A dream come true.

And he had bought her the theatre, after all. He was the reason her name was above the door of the theatre she had come to as a child, the one that had made her want to be a star. A childhood production of Noel Streatfeild's *Ballet Shoes* had set her on the path and now here she was, a Dame for her services to the dramatic arts. And tomorrow she would become immortal. Because of the pantomime, yes. Because it was her comeback after years away from the stage, yes. But also because of what was going to happen onstage, thanks to Beatrice's carefully laid plans.

She inhaled the sharp sea air and stepped into the street. And that was when she heard the screech of wheels, the revving of an engine. A black SUV was speeding down the road, aiming straight for her; it was going to plough her down.

As she flung herself backwards she saw that the driver's face was obscured beneath a black beanie and shades. Beatrice landed heavily against a railing, clinging on to hold herself up. She exhaled, her heart beating too fast, her mouth dry.

'Dame Beatrice. Are you all right, madam?' Carl burst out of the building and was at her side, taking her hand, steadying her.

'Yes, thank you, Carl.' For a second, dizziness threatened, but Beatrice had gritted her teeth through worse in the past few months. She pushed him away and stood up straight. That had been unexpected. But she had survived. And if you put cats amongst pigeons, you had to expect whatever trouble came next. She inhaled deeply. It would take more than a dangerous driver to take Beatrice Butler down. She had never felt more liberated. More free. She held her head high and marched towards her first meeting of the day.

6

AMBER

The assistant director's words left a deafening silence in the auditorium. Amber looked around, alert, sitting up in her seat, checking the faces of the audience around her, trying to see if anyone was reacting in a way that might indicate guilt. Because Amber knew, from a *Saga* magazine she had read in the dentist last week, that Beatrice Butler was in stellar health. She was still hiking, leading ballet classes and travelling around the world. So, even though Jaxon had not mentioned murder, Amber suspected foul play. After all, she was pretty sure that Dame Beatrice had been the person she had overheard in the toilet, arguing on the phone, saying that nothing would stop her. Maybe a killer had been at the other end of the line and, as always, Amber wanted to be the one who got to the bottom of the mystery.

It had always been like this for Amber. She loved uncovering secrets, solving puzzles, catching the bad guys. Back in her teenage years, Amber had experimented with going off the rails and got back on track when she was caught climbing a water tower and taken into the police station to be cautioned. Brought up in the care system, with a new foster home every few months, she had struggled to find her way before that night. Her wild behaviour became a hot topic amongst the various foster carers and social workers who tried to help her. In the end it had been Jeanie's dad who had shown her that she could choose a different future. When he was called in as duty solicitor after the water tower incident, he had stood up for her, and

Amber had ended up becoming part of the Martin family for her remaining years at sixth form college. So it was really thanks to him that Amber had completed more than two decades on the local force, working first as a PC and then as a detective. And now she used those skills to run her own agency, The Bad Girls Detective Agency, employing her two best friends, Jeanie and Clio.

Next to Amber, Jeanie's children were not happy that the show hadn't started yet. There was a persistent squeaking as Yumi started to bounce up and down in her seat, while Jack started a low-level whimper that set Amber's teeth on edge. Around them, people started to whisper about Beatrice's death, voices low, as if they were struggling to believe what Jaxon had just said. The man himself had disappeared, hopefully to call the police, although in Amber's experience they might be a long time coming. At the end of the row, a lady with a huge grey bun appeared to have fainted, sliding sideways until she was only saved from ending up in the aisle by the intervention of her husband, who reached out to grab her by the arm and resurrect her. The woman blinked, clearly disorientated, before saying, 'Is it true?'

Amber could sit still no longer. Before she even knew what she was doing, she was on her feet, ready to investigate, every motion and instinct honed by her years as a detective. She had to get behind the scenes and see what she could find out. She must make the most of the golden hour, when the trail was so fresh it was easier to follow the clues – those precious minutes before the killer had a chance to cover their tracks.

She leant down, whispering into Jeanie's ear. 'I'm going to go and have a look. Just to see if I can be helpful at all.'

'You can't resist a crime scene, can you?' Jeanie gave a smile, while trying desperately to contain her children, who were visibly annoyed now at the lack of action. She was half-standing, taking Jack by the waist and bringing him onto her lap, starting to bounce him up and down while optimistically singing, 'The Wheels on the Bus.'

Amber moved past her, turning back to say, 'Neither can you.'

'Not sure that it's that child-friendly back there. Murder doesn't agree with minors.' Jeanie sighed. 'I'll try to keep them entertained in here. But...' Amber could see the glint in her eyes. 'Let me know what you find. And I can always start doing some online research, if there's anything juicy going on. I heard Beatrice arguing with a couple of people backstage earlier – a woman and a man with a Welsh accent. I got here just after six thirty – which means she was definitely alive until very recently.'

'Thank you.' Amber grinned. One of her favourite things about running the detective agency was how much her two best friends had fallen in love with solving mysteries. They got such a buzz from tracking missing people, from catching errant husbands, or even, in three separate cases, finding killers. The agency had started by accident when Clio had been prime suspect in her ex, Gary's, murder, with the three best friends uniting to find the real killer and save Clio from jail. And now the agency was going from strength to strength, with a waiting list lasting well into next year.

'MAMA.' Jack's voice could shatter glass. Everyone in the auditorium turned to look at him, and even the chandelier that hung above the stalls seemed to rattle in reply.

It was time to disappear. Amber leant down, cupping her hand over Jeanie's ear. 'Keep an eye on what's going on in here, okay? Let me know if anyone disappears suddenly, or deliberately creates a distraction or anything.' She gestured towards the flailing children. 'If you can?'

'I'll do my best.' Jeanie nodded, pushing her curls out of her flushed face. 'I think my two have got the distractions covered though.' She eyed Jack warily as he elbowed her in the ribs. He was bouncing up and down on her knee while Yumi was busy trying to pick the metal-plated seat number off the armrest. 'I'll try to keep my eyes peeled for anything suspicious. You go, Amber. Go see what's happening.'

'On it.' Amber was now moving along the row, nimble in her trainers and black skinny jeans, making a mental note never to buy a Christmas pudding headband like the one being sported by the woman across the aisle. God, she hated Christmas. It had always been the worst day growing up, no matter how lovely the foster family or how kind the staff at the children's home. Her childhood Christmas gifts had always been so depressing: always something useful rather than fun. Her worst one ever was a pair of brown moccasin slippers, which she was convinced had belonged to the recently deceased mum of her then-foster dad. No, Christmas was a day for family, a family that Amber had not possessed until this year, when Melissa had tracked her down. This year Amber knew that she would not be allowed to hide away.

An usher with oiled brown hair blocked her path when she reached the exit. 'Madam, you need to stay in here.' Sweat glistened on his brow.

'Why?' Amber tried to push past but he stopped her with a surprisingly agile sidestep.

Amber was about to remonstrate with him when a woman in a 'Going Sprout-Sprout' red T-shirt bumped into her, completely failing to apologise.

The woman addressed the usher, and Amber recognised her from a recent WI meeting. Amber had been guest speaker, telling them all about the secrets of crime solving. They had lapped it up, asking some of the most challenging questions Amber had faced in her entire career, which had included multiple press conferences for cases that were not going to plan. You messed with the WI at your peril.

Now, the woman's voice rose. 'You must let me out. I need to use the facilities.'

The usher shook his head. 'I can't, I'm afraid. The police are on their way, and we've been told to hold everyone here.' He folded his arms, and Amber could see a light down on his upper lip. He couldn't be more than eighteen and he was about to have the wrath of the Sunshine Sands WI unleashed upon his head. Amber didn't envy him. With the woman still remonstrating, Amber chanced her luck, flashing her fake police ID at him and successfully passing through the heavy exit door and back out into the foyer. Despite her full roster of clients, she couldn't resist being one of the first on scene tonight. The death of a local legend would always be worth a look, just in case she could spot something that might help to cast a light on who might have killed them. Not that this was definitely a murder, of course. But just in case...

In the foyer she glanced around, assessing the level of scrutiny going on. As she had guessed, chaos reigned. The bar staff were all whispering to each other, paying no attention to what was going on around them. The front doors had been shut but not bolted, and several members of the audience escaped into the open air as Amber was watching. She debated setting up a serious lockdown, with a manned perimeter, to stop further suspects from leaving the building, but decided instead to get backstage and get a feel for what was happening. From what Clio had been saying about the rehearsals, the murderer was highly likely to be in the cast or the crew, so that was where she would focus.

She knew from the times she had come to meet Clio that the dressing rooms (too small, too dingy, in Clio's disparaging view) were positioned around the back behind the stage, next to a dysfunctional septic tank and above a huge cellar that ran the entire width of the theatre. Clio had always joked that there were probably bodies buried down there, but now, maybe there actually might be. It was obvious to any passer-by that the Beatrice Butler Theatre was crumbling to such a degree that total collapse might happen at any moment – and it could be that a beam had fallen, or that Beatrice Butler had fallen down some rotting stairs and was now in a crumpled heap at the bottom. Killed by her own theatre – what a dramatically appropriate ending for a woman like her.

Amber looked right and left. No police, no one looking. She ran for a side door and went straight through, unchallenged, and began to sprint down the corridor that led to the dressing rooms, pulling a pair of latex gloves out of her back pocket as she ran. She had beaten the police to a murder scene three times before, each time catching the killer before them. It wouldn't hurt to do so a fourth time, would it? She just needed a quick look round before they arrived.

The dingy corridor smelt of camomile tea and sewage, with doors opening off it at regular intervals. A mouse skittered into a hole just in front of her and all in all the scene was just as unglamorous as Clio had described. She wondered where Beatrice's body had been found – in her dressing room, or backstage; who had found her; why they had gone in to see her. Amber looked right and left, hearing hushed voices ahead, and switching on the torch on her phone to scan the ground as she ran. Anything could be a clue. Everything she saw could mean something, or absolutely nothing at all. Amber was already doing what she was born to do: starting to store away snapshots in her memory, before piecing them all together later into a murder theory that included means, motive and opportunity.

She kept walking fast, hoping that nobody would try and stop her. She held her head high, exuding authority and purpose, as she rounded a bend and headed down the left fork. Her feet bounced against scuffed grey carpet, while along the slightly mouldy walls to either side were hung signed pictures of various theatrical grandees who had played roles here during the theatre's heyday. Once upon a time it had been a mecca for London's theatrical elite but now it had an air of dejection, the only historical building still standing in the area around the pier, surrounded by shops offering discount goods and an ever-expanding housing estate.

Amber reached a door, which said 'Actors and Production Team Only'. Again, she went through it, hoping she was heading the right way. Where was the body? It was like the Tardis back here. Amber felt like she was in a maze with no map and no idea where the middle might be. She followed her gut instinct, rounding another corner to arrive at a larger dressing room with stars on the half-open door. This must be it, a fact confirmed when she entered the room and saw a man prostrate on the floor, sobs racking his body.

Above him, lying sideways across a mustard-yellow chaise-longue, was Beatrice Butler. Amber stood for a moment, staring at the body, as if in tribute. Beatrice's face was so familiar, despite the fact that Amber only ever went to the theatre to watch Clio, and rarely watched any TV that didn't involve true crime. But Beatrice's face had become part of the national DNA, like Sir David Attenborough, so it would have been in Amber's mind even if it hadn't been given top billing on the pantomime poster outside the theatre. On that poster, Beatrice had a wand in her hand and mischief in her eyes, her cheeks glittering and her hair sprayed a sparkling silver.

Now, all that life was gone. Beatrice lay on her side, half her skull missing, her red nails matching the lipstick on her slack mouth. Her long glittering dress, which Amber presumed was her Fairy Moonshine costume, was rucked up beneath her, exposing her calves in their sparkling silver tights. Her face, or what remained of it, was white, her skin already sporting a waxy sheen beneath the jagged crater in her forehead. At her feet was a small silver pistol, clearly abandoned in something of a hurry next to a widening pool of blood by the chaise-longue. Amber wondered if the killer may have been disturbed, and looked down at the sobbing man. Maybe he had seen something.

Amber gave a deep sigh as she stared down at the crime scene. Christmas or no Christmas, it had happened again. The three of them were once more hunting a killer. Beatrice Butler, grande dame of British theatre, had, quite clearly, been murdered.

7

AMBER

Aware that the police would arrive any minute and ban her instantly from the scene, Amber started taking pictures of everything around her: a white plate bearing an untouched mince pie; an unsigned contract; a chaotic pile of papers on the dressing table; a glass of sherry, again untouched; and the remains of something that had been burned in the sink. But most of all, Amber looked at the pistol: at the jewels on the handle; wondering why there was mistletoe and tinsel around the barrel; wondering who had picked up the weapon and blasted Beatrice's skull away; who had hated Beatrice enough to end her time on earth.

'Amber. You made it. I knew you would.' Clio emerged from a walk-in cupboard in the corner of the dressing room, already sporting her own pair of latex gloves (Amber had trained her team well), wearing what was certainly one of the least flattering costumes that Amber had ever seen. She stopped, clocking Amber's expression and doing a twirl in her hideous hessian sack. 'Yes, I know, I look like a putrid potato. No need to take the piss. Let's focus here. Someone's killed one of the greatest actresses of our time, and I want to know who, even if she was a cow.' Clio started leafing through the mound of papers on the dressing table.

'On the case.' Amber indicated the weeping man at her feet, uncomfortable with such an extravagant display of emotion. 'Who's this?'

'Gawain. Props and set design.' Clio's knee clicked as she dropped to his side. 'Gawain, I know this is really hard. It's tough for all of us. But, do you think you could go and cry outside please? You're a bit in the way down there.'

'I can't believe she's gone.' The man spoke in a deep baritone. His face was blotchy and pale, his eyes dull with what looked like genuine grief. 'It's just so devastating.'

Clio gently touched his shoulder. 'I get it. It's a shock. Your first dead body is a big moment. Mine was my ex, and I puked all over the place, so I feel your pain. I mean, she was horrible to you, and sure, she insulted you every single day that you worked on this production, especially when that light nearly killed her yesterday, but still...'

Gawain howled again. 'She was just trying to get the best out of me.'

'If you say so.' Clio supported him as she lifted the man to his feet, putting her arms around his shoulders to steady him. 'Now, this is a crime scene, and you need to go and find the rest of the team and wait with them. Okay?'

Amber raised her hand to stop him. 'Can I just ask you a few questions first?'

Gawain nodded, still racked by sobs, groping in his pocket for a tissue. Amber waited until he had found one. 'When did you arrive in this room, Gawain?'

His eyes glistened. 'I heard the shot, and I came running.'

'And what time was that?'

'Just before seven-thirty. Winnie asked me to come.'

'She's the stage manager.' Clio threw this over her shoulder as she continued examining papers.

Gawain blew his nose. 'She'd done the five-minute call, but Beatrice hadn't appeared. Everyone else was waiting in the wings, but she wasn't there, so Winnie sent me to find her.'

Amber was thinking rapidly. 'Everyone else was in the wings at that point? The entire cast?'

'Yes.' He took a shuddering breath. 'Only just, though. They all arrived around the same time, now I come to think about it – only about a minute before I went to look for Beatrice.'

So any of the cast could have done it. Including Clio. Again.

Gawain dabbed ineffectually at his eyes. 'And I came here and... there she was. Just like this.' He threw his head back in a howl of anguish.

'Okay, okay.' Clio patted his shoulder.

Amber eyed him carefully. He genuinely seemed like a man in shock. 'And then what happened?'

'Clio came and found me. They needed me to get on the lighting desk and start the show.'

Clio nodded. 'True. I sprinted down here and there she was. So I called the police.' She pulled Gawain to his feet. 'And did you see anyone else hanging around, in the corridor or outside the room?'

'No.' Gawain wiped his face with his hand. 'No, I didn't.'

'Thank you so much.' Clio led him to the door. 'You've been amazing.'

He reached the corridor and hesitated. 'Let me know if there's anything I can do. Anything to help catch whoever did this.'

'We will.' Clio pushed him gently down the corridor, before turning and making her way back into the dressing room. She peered at the mirror, which was adorned with fairy lights, while the walls were covered with pictures of Beatrice in various productions or socialising with her famous friends. 'God, how the hell did she know Lady Gaga?'

Amber shrugged.

'Oh, and there she is with Michael Ball.' Clio shrugged. 'Mind you, everyone knew Michael Ball back in the day.'

Amber needed her friend to focus. They didn't have long. 'What have you found so far?' Amber moved towards the walk-in wardrobe.

Clio puffed air out of her cheeks. 'Not a lot. There's a huge hat box in the back of the wardrobe, full of old diaries and stuff. Beatrice writes a page a day, no matter what, and it's pretty scurrilous stuff. They're chronological, except one is missing – 1975. She writes an entry every day of every year from what I can see – it goes all the way back to 1970, possibly further, only I didn't get a chance to look that far as I was trying to get Gawain to leave so I could concentrate. There are loads of cuttings books too – like the one Melissa has about you, Amber.'

Amber cringed. Her half-sister's tendency to glorify Amber's career made her cheeks burn. She needed to change the subject. 'Who else has come into the room, besides Gawain?'

'Jaxon came in, after I texted him. He nearly fainted, before realising he needed to take charge.'

'Yeah, he made the announcement to the audience. He's wearing a pork-pie hat and spectacles, right?' Amber started to look through the clothes that were hanging up in the wardrobe. Fur coats, silk scarves, a grey jumper dress scattered with discrete silver stars. Vertiginous high heels were stacked up on the floor in varying shades of black, while a rack of jewellery was attached to the inner door, with strings of pearls, a golden locket and countless sets of earrings. 'Jeanie's keeping an eye on what the people in the audience are doing – seeing if anyone is acting suspiciously.'

'Good luck to her. I'm sure that Yumi and Jack are putting on a show.' Clio arched her eyebrows. 'They're at peak toddler right now and it's nearly 8 p.m. Who needs a panto when you've got that kind of crazy in the building?' She walked over to the body, leaning down. 'Hang on. Where's her ruby ring?'

'What ring?'

'She has – I mean she had – this massive ruby ring that her husband gave her back in their glory days. She never takes it off. I used to think it was a torture technique for her cast, because the light hits it and it's as bright as an interrogation lamp, straight between the eyes. You just say yes to anything she says, you know, just to get that light out of your face. Sylvia – the costume designer – she says it's Cartier and worth at least half a million. And she should know. She was involved in organising that exhibition of the Crown Jewels a while back at the Tower of London and she worked on a production of *Evita* and had to source a ton of costume jewellery for that. If anyone can size up the cost of something, it's her.'

Amber nodded, her interest quickening. Money like that was a strong motive for murder. They both looked around, but no ring was to be found. It had completely vanished. She looked at Beatrice again, examining her more closely. 'Are those marks, around her neck? Like someone's tried to strangle her?' She put her head on one side.

'Where?' Clio turned round from dressing table, where she was now sifting through lipsticks, eyeshadows and various bottles of perfume.

'Look.' Amber indicated the sides of Beatrice's neck, where there was a faint redness to either side, mottling her alabaster skin.

Clio frowned. 'Well, if someone did try to strangle her then they didn't try very hard.'

Amber took pictures, convinced she was right. Then she went back into the wardrobe and took a quick look at the piles of diaries. She longed to take them away, but to do so would be a step too far. She was still enough of a police officer to know that she must leave everything at the crime scene. She didn't want her ex-boss, Marco Santini, on her case, giving her grief for interfering in his investigation. As she came out, she saw a bottle of pills lying on the windowsill, and she photographed that too. Heart medication? Or something else?

Clio turned back to face her. 'There's nothing on the dressing table. Just a load of old make-up and hair products.' She put her head on one side, considering. 'You know, whoever did it must have been pretty fast. I wonder if they planned it?'

'Jeanie mentioned that she heard a woman arguing with Beatrice earlier. And then a man was in there as she left. Welsh accent, so probably Gawain. Funny how he didn't mention that just now, isn't it?'

'Gawain?' Clio's face clouded. 'But he seemed so upset. And Jeanie...? Oh yes! When she was backstage looking for the kids.' She nodded. 'I wonder which woman it was: Kylie or Sylvia.' She took a long breath. 'Or maybe Winnie, the stage manager, did it!' Clio peered at the pistol. 'That looks quite similar to the pistol that's used in the show, when Jack is pretending to fire at me, and the whole audience is hating on me, because I'm the baddie.'

'Who do you think is most likely to have done it, then?'

Clio shrugged. 'Give them the opportunity and a fair wind and anyone could have done it. She was a total cow. A dictator. A control freak. A name dropper. A fake, a liar. She was a character assassin too. She lied to agents, lied to casting directors, blocked people getting roles and jobs.' She moved around the room, taking photos, as Amber had done. The Bad Girls were never ones to let an opportunity to amass evidence pass them by.

'You know, I've never met anyone with so many people queuing up to kill them. Not since my rotten ex-husband, anyway.' Clio stopped speaking suddenly and Amber looked up from the back of the chaise-longue. 'Oh my God.' Clio's voice had dropped an octave. 'Look at this. Look what I've found.'

Amber got to her feet and walked over. Not that she needed to, really. Clio had lifted up a mirror that formed part of the dressing table. And written on the glass were some red letters that were so big that they could be read from the other side of the room.

The letters spelt the following words:

Your time is over, bitch.

Clio turned to Amber. 'See? I told you. Everyone hated her.'

'Did they?' A deep voice came from the doorway. 'I can't wait to hear more about that. That green skin suits you, Clio. Very Elphaba.' DI Marco Santini smiled proudly around the room, as if impressed by his own modern day cultural references. He looked genuinely disappointed when neither Clio nor Amber smiled back.

He made a shooing gesture with his hands. 'So, you two had better go back into the foyer with everyone else, hadn't you? Leave the professionals to it, yes?'

Amber gritted her teeth, feeling a familiar buzz of irritation building as her nemesis and ex-boss walked into the room. He leant towards her as she walked past. 'You'd best run along and play with your little friends, leave the big boys to it.' He smiled showing yellowing teeth, and in that moment, Amber forgot all her sensible decisions and her determination to focus on building her own business. In that moment, with the dead body at her side, hearing the phrase 'leave the big boys to it', she decided that she and her team were going to solve this case no matter what Marco had planned.

Amber was going to beat him to the killer, and nothing was going to stop her.

8
CLIO

Clio knew before Amber said anything that her friend had decided to solve this case. Amber always got the same look when she was working on something, a kind of brightness to her eyes, a set line to her lips. At school she had always had to be the winner in any fight, any race, any limbo competition at an end-of-term school disco. And nothing got Amber's blood up like a tussle with DI Marco Santini, the man who had once fired her and who then had tried to put Clio on the hook for a murder she hadn't committed. Later, he had tried to rehire Amber, only for her to say no and go off and start her own detective agency instead. Proving him wrong was catnip to Amber, and so far, the Bad Girls Detective Agency had consistently come out ahead in every murder case they had taken on, without access to any of the resources the police had at their disposal, like the Police National Computer, post-mortem results or forensics.

Clio whispered in Amber's ear as a young officer shepherded them along to the foyer, where the rest of the cast and the audience were waiting. 'I've got an idea.'

Amber leant towards her. 'Is it better than the time that you bought that old camper van at Glastonbury, when you were too drunk to notice it didn't have wheels?'

Clio pulled a face. Amber was never going to let her forget about that. Her friend could be so unforgiving sometimes. 'Yes.' She sighed. 'But Vivian the van was great in the end, wasn't she? Do you remember when we took her to the Isle of Wight?'

'The time she broke down on the ferry?' Amber rolled her eyes.

'Did she?'

'Yes. But you probably don't remember as I was the one who went all the way back to the mainland with her, while you hitched a ride in someone else's camper van and spent the next three days locked in his arms.'

'Oh yes. So I did.' Clio felt herself smile at the memory of Stefan. He had been tanned, with long, curly hair and piercings in very exciting places. She missed those short, intense affairs, those romantic moments: firelight, sand, a cigarette glowing in the darkness, hands entwining. Her latest fling had barely made it to second base. There had been some lovely dinners and some laughs, but ultimately, Adrian the insurance broker had seemed more excited about his upcoming Ironman race than about getting to know Clio better.

She sighed. It was dispiriting sometimes, being alone. Especially with Bez and Tiara so obviously on cloud nine all the time.

'So come on.' Amber arched an eyebrow. 'Focus. We're going to be split up in a minute and you said you had an idea?'

Clio clicked back into the present. They were nearly in the foyer now, just passing the side of the theatre, and she could hear that the audience were not happy about the night's events. They had come expecting a pantomime Dame, some *'Oh, no she didn't's'*, a comedy animal, some stupid baddies chasing each other around the stage and a national treasure in a fairy costume, pulling some kind of a pantomime happy ending out of the end of her sparkly wand. Instead, all they had got for their money was a real-life dead body and an evening trapped in a drafty theatre where the snacks had probably already run out.

'So...' Amber kept close to her as they pushed their way through the heavy door to arrive in the foyer. It was now full of police who were taping off the entrance so that nobody could come in or out. The gravity of the blue and white tape made an uncomfortable contrast with the pantomime posters above it with their purple background, gold lettering and the smiling faces of the cast. 'What's your big idea?'

'What big idea?'

'The one you had just now? Before the van diversion?'

'Oh, sorry. I thought I'd told you already.' Clio frowned in frustration. 'God, my HRT patches aren't working that well, are they?'

'Are you actually sticking them to your body? Because they only work if you do that.'

Clio grinned. 'You know me too well, Amber.'

Amber nodded. 'Yes, I do. That's what three decades of friendship will do for you.'

Clio grimaced. 'Three decades. God, no wonder I look so old.'

Amber smiled. 'Dressed up in that sack, you do.'

'You said you wouldn't laugh at me!'

'No.' Amber wagged a finger. 'You asked me not to laugh at you. Not the same thing.'

Clio sighed. 'I can't believe you're not going to get to see my big dance. It's the stuff of dreams. Next stop, the Royal Variety Performance.'

'Poor King Charles. Hasn't he had enough to deal with recently?'

'Hey.' Clio hit her on the arm. 'Don't be so disrespectful. The *Sunshine Sands Gazette* was going to say that I was the best villain they'd ever seen on the stage at The Beatrice Butler Theatre.' She laughed. 'My career could have really taken off, you know? A lead role in a Netflix series. Or Amazon Prime. I'm not picky.'

'Hey. You work for me now. What's your plan, Clio? Quick – before they split us up!'

'Listen.' Clio put a hand on her friend's arm. The buzz from the auditorium was growing louder. The audience had been imprisoned for a while now, and Clio presumed they had gone from surprise to horror to 'Oh no, I'm going to miss my train and there's no one to feed the dog.'

Clio spoke fast. 'I am guessing they'll keep the cast back for questioning, to help them to establish a timeline of what happened before she was killed. Right?'

'Right.' Amber nodded eagerly, as the young officer came to a halt a few metres in front of them, discussing something with a colleague. They only had seconds left. 'And?'

'So, clearly one of us needs to be in the interview room so we can hear how the interviews go and what everyone gives away about themselves. That way, we can keep up with what the police are finding out, yes? Because obviously Marco isn't going to share anything, is he?'

'Yes. But how? What's the plan?' Amber eyed her attentively, and Clio felt a beat of pride. She always liked impressing her friend and boss. A compliment from her was hard to get but worth all the more when it came.

She leant closer. 'So why don't you hide inside the cow costume?'

Amber snorted. 'You what?'

Clio shrugged. 'You heard me. The police are bound to use the rehearsal room as it's the biggest space, the furthest from the crime scene and the only backstage room that doesn't really smell of sewage, so, I thought we could get you in there. I can just tell the police that I need the loo, mutter about women's issues – that'll scare them, and then I'll move the costume in there and leave it in the back corner, furthest from the door, so you can climb into it and listen to the interviews. No problem.'

'And you don't think they'll check inside the costume?'

'No. Why would they? Plus, you always said Marco doesn't do detail.'

Amber pulled a face. 'But won't I look a bit – um – backless?'

'What do you mean?' Clio could see the police officer coming back towards her.

Amber coughed. 'Well, you know. I can't be both halves of a cow, can I? So the cow will have no legs, will she?'

Clio thought for a moment. 'Well, like I said, the costume will just be on the floor. All you need to do is find it and get inside and lie down in it. Like it's a blanket, just a cow-shaped one.'

Amber swallowed. 'Um. I'm not sure about this. It's pretty dodgy. If I get caught, I'll get a right bollocking. I could even be charged.'

'Marco's not going to charge you – he knows that you have too much dirt on him.' Clio spoke in an urgent whisper. 'Oh come on, Amber, this isn't like you. You're normally the one leaping out of insanely high towers or jumping onto moving boats or attacking killers with only a wooden stick to defend yourself. This is just getting inside a cow costume. It's easy! Just do it! Otherwise, we have no chance of cracking this case. We'll never be able to do it.'

'You'll never be able to do what?' Ross Jones had appeared at Clio's side, his hair pulled back ready for his pantomime dame wig, his face fully made up with red hearts on his cheeks and a perfect red Cupid's bow painted on to his mouth. He had on a full corset, frilly bloomers, a light blue dress decorated in silver clouds and white high heels with a purple buckle. Yet beneath the make-up his face was ashen, and he looked far more upset than Clio would have believed possible, given the feelings about Beatrice that he had expressed so regularly in rehearsal.

'Nothing.' Clio gave Amber a final nod and turned and walked with Ross, following the officer across the foyer. 'Have you heard the news, Ross?'

'Oh my God, I can't believe it, Clio.' He took her by the arm, his fingers biting so hard that she had to gently remove them. 'She's gone. Beatrice Butler. I thought she'd be with us forever. And Gawain said that she's been murdered? I mean, I know we all had our moments with her, but I never thought anyone would actually go through with it.'

Clio nodded, puzzled about where all this regret was coming from. This was quite a change of tone from Ross, but he appeared totally sincere.

He put his hand over his eyes. 'It's just, I can't take it in. Who on earth would have done such a thing?'

'I don't know.' Clio peered more closely at him. Was that a tear rolling down his cheek? He wasn't that good an actor, as she had seen on countless occasions over the rehearsal period, so maybe he was really grieving. Had there been some extra depth to his relationship with Beatrice that she had not known about? Should he be on their list of suspects?

He swallowed, his Adam's apple bobbing as he did so. 'They're just clearing the rehearsal room now so they can talk to us one by one. They're going to interview us – it's just like on *CSI*. I was in my dressing room when it happened, so I don't think I'll be much help, but...'

Clio saw a tiny frond of mistletoe on his dress and went to pull it off, before remembering that the same plant had been wrapped around the barrel of the pistol. Could it have been Ross? And if so, why? Because Beatrice had cut his big song, or was something else going on? Clio itched to find out. As he talked on and on about how upset he was, Clio wondered whether he was slightly over-egging his grief. They reached the rehearsal room and the police directed them to wait in two of the dressing rooms nearby. Clio sat down on the one chair, feeling like she was back in the holding cell at Sunshine Sands Police Station. She ran through the cast in her head and resolved to keep an eye on all of them until they had found the killer. One of them must have done it. One of them had murdered their director and Clio was determined to find out who.

Speaking of which, she needed to move the costume. She stuck her head out of the room and saw that the coast was clear as all of the police had been gathered for some kind of briefing at the end of the corridor. All Clio had to do was sneak into the rehearsal room and move the costume into the corner, as promised. She crept along the corridor, her heart hammering as she grabbed both halves of the costume from the rack outside the rehearsal room and opened the door. She exhaled as she saw that no one was there. She scurried across and dropped the costume onto the floor, the fear of being caught making her breath tight in her chest.

Hyperventilating, she made her way back to her allotted dressing room. The police were still being briefed, and she crept inside, hoping that Amber could make it into the rehearsal room, that she could hide underneath the costume and that whatever she heard would prove useful in catching Beatrice's killer. Then, as her hand was on the door handle, she heard a scream.

She halted, her heart beating hard in her chest.

The scream had sounded very much like Jeanie.

9

BEATRICE BUTLER

09.25: Ten hours until her death

Beatrice Butler looked around the Bean Me Up cafe, wincing inwardly at the sticky red tables, the stewed coffee in the tarnished silver canteen by the checkout, the stained checked apron of the proprietor. Much as she enjoyed berating the deficiencies of the modern world, such as the strange societal tendency to go cashless or to walk along the street staring at tiny screens, being in here felt to Beatrice like travelling back in time in the very worst of ways. Her hair would be smelling of chip fat for weeks to come and she was sure that the man behind the counter hadn't washed his hands before serving the only other customer his decidedly greasy fry-up.

The person that Beatrice was due to see was late, giving Beatrice far too much time to notice everything that was wrong with their meeting venue. She was not used to being the one left waiting, usually preferring to arrive at least ten minutes after the arranged time, sweeping into the venue wafting apologies and perfume, always forgiven for her tardiness simply because of who she was. Sitting on a wobbly plastic chair nursing a revolting cup of stewed tea was absolutely not Beatrice's usual style. Normally, she met her friends at high-end places such as Claridge's or The Ritz or, at a push, The Wolseley. She had never come in here – had never even dreamt of it until she was hatching her grand plan and was forced out of her comfort zone. She examined the plastic menu again and shuddered, seeing pickled eggs listed under Side Dishes. Above it, under Mains, was the Ultimate Bacon Butty, aka a heart attack on a plate.

She looked up, reading the posters on the walls, sighing inwardly as she saw a council notice poster about the planning process for the new housing development, planned just around the corner from her theatre. She was tempted to rip the poster down and dunk it in her terrible tea. It might make the disgusting liquid taste better. The thought made her smile, and she wished Florian were across the table from her to complain with. He had never been one to shy away from a good bitch. He had always stayed up to see her when she got back from the theatre, a steaming mug of camomile tea ready beside her chair, the fire lit. He had sat opposite her, sipping his whisky, as she told him all the backstage gossip, his eyes alight, his hearty laugh ringing out as she shared every salacious detail. Even though she had betrayed him, he had always been her best audience, her number one fan. It was just as well he had never found out what she had done.

A girl stumbled into the cafe, headphones on, puffa coat done up to her chin, her eyes never leaving her mobile phone as she ordered. As she walked out again with some foul-smelling coffee, Beatrice began to wonder if the person she was meeting was going to stand her up. If so, it would be a first, and not in a good way. Beatrice was always careful to be publicly humble, always thanking everyone around her when she went up onstage to collect an Olivier award, or a BAFTA, even her damehood from the late Queen herself. It turned out that Her Majesty was such a fan of Beatrice's *Top Deck* character that she had apparently had a VHS player installed in the Palace just so she could watch the programme. She had been positively skittish when they had talked, but Beatrice was used to these reactions and had navigated it all with her usual grace and charm.

The bell tinkled as the door to the cafe swung open again. The prickling on Beatrice's neck told her that it must be the person she was here to meet. They weren't normally someone who gave her any trouble, but she couldn't take any chances today. She arranged herself in a suitably intimidating style, her spine straight, her eyes fierce, taking comfort from knowing that the pistol was hidden in her handbag for later. It was her husband who had given it to her, during his time directing *Macbeth* at the Old Vic, a time when he had gone more than a little insane, telling Beatrice she must be able to protect herself 'in case the three witches came for her'. She had never used it, of course, but had kept it locked away, a memento of his love for her.

She fixed a fierce stare on the person who walked in, who was wearing a smile far wider than the occasion should allow. Beatrice held their gaze as they sat down in front of her, raincoat crumpled, hair dark with the December rain, hands folded in front of them on the table. They smelt strongly of wet dog, an unfortunate scent, which Beatrice guessed was emanating from their thick woollen jumper.

She blinked at them severely, pushing her tea to the side.

She opened her mouth, ready to declaim the lines she had prepared the night before. They were lifted from an old detective play, but her companion would never know that. 'I—'

Her companion smiled. 'Aren't you going to thank me for coming?'

Beatrice paused, temporarily lost for words, an experience entirely new to her. 'I...'

The person leant forwards. 'You invited me here, after all. I'm obviously not considered worthy of your usual haunts.'

Beatrice needed to regain her customary ascendancy, so she pointed a finger across the table, aimed squarely at her companion's chest. 'Now, just you listen to me. I am here to tell you to stop this harassment. To tell you that this thing you think you know about me, this lie about my past, about my marriage, about who I really am...' She realised she was shaking and exhaled to steady herself. She didn't want to think back to the time when she was little Betty, stuck in a grim slate primary school building by the beach, always desperate to escape. She was gone by the age of sixteen, running away to London, doing anything she could to pay her way, before landing in *Jack and the Beanstalk*, meeting Florian and then getting into the Royal Academy of Dramatic Art. She had never, ever looked back, never regretted her past, and she wasn't going to start now.

The clock was ticking here, and she needed to get this meeting wrapped up. She was aware that the second dress rehearsal was starting soon, aware of how much the cast would need her today, how much they would look to her, Beatrice Butler, their director, to keep the show on the road. She was not going to be blackmailed by anyone; she was not going to let this presumptuous lowlife get in her way.

She dropped her voice to a hiss. *Less is more*, as darling Maggie Smith used to say. 'I am here to tell you to stop. Stop coming to my apartment, stop threatening me, just stop.'

'Why should I listen to you?'

Beatrice narrowed her eyes. 'Who do you think you are, talking to me like that? Don't you know I was friends with Olivier?'

'So what?'

Beatrice closed her eyes for a moment, struggling to contain her horror.

Her companion tipped an indecent amount of sugar into the coffee that the proprietor had brought to the table. 'But I have heard of a certain Jamie Byngham.' They started to stir using a filthy teaspoon. 'Ring any bells?'

'None whatsoever,' Beatrice lied, raising her chin defiantly. It would take more than this fool to break her.

'Really?' Her companion sat back, seemingly relaxed. 'Oh, I think you have heard of him. In fact, I think you know him rather well. He was a big director in the West End, back in the day. Back when you were young, Beatrice. Can you remember that far back?'

Beatrice ignored the insult. She had heard worse. She had worked with Richard Harris during his many drinking years – nothing could shock her after that. She waited, giving the person across the table her finest arctic stare, once described as 'so cold I had to put my coat on' by Benedict Nightingale, the greatest theatre critic of them all. She knew what this person was here for, and there was absolutely no way they were going to get what they wanted.

'You're a cool customer aren't you, Beatrice? Every inch the unflappable Dame. Every inch the star. It must be nice being you, getting lovely greetings in the street, appearing on *Graham Norton* every time you've got a memoir out, happily married for all those years.'

'What's your point here? Because I've told you before – the answer is no.'

'Is it, though?'

'Meaning?' Beatrice was getting tired of this.

Yet more sugar was added. Then they finally got to the point.

'Beatrice. We all have our secrets, don't we?'

'No.' Beatrice held her chin high, holding the person's gaze. Maybe she could bluff this out. She had done it before, even when it had been her husband asking the questions.

The person arched their eyebrows. 'Oh, I think even you have a secret or two.'

Beatrice stayed silent and wondered if this meeting would ever be over. It was right down there with the time she had been rejected for Princess Leia in *Star Wars*. She had been so close, her agent encouraging her every step of the way, and then that wretched Carrie Fisher had stolen it from under her nose. Beatrice had been sure to send her an unpleasant item of mail every year until she died. Some tasks were a pleasure, not a chore, weren't they?

The person opposite her gave a low whistle. 'Wow, you're a tough crowd, aren't you, Beatrice?'

'One doesn't get to the top by being a pushover.'

'No, but you might get to the top by lying back and thinking of England.'

Beatrice couldn't help flinching at this. The words pulled the lid off a box buried deep inside her mind: a distant memory of a silk kimono, a candle in her hand, her lips on his. Soft sheets, the fizz of champagne, wallpaper decorated with dark pink roses. His hand in hers, leading her up a wide staircase towards his suite on the top floor of the hotel. His voice, so low, with that gentle Scottish accent. The scrape of cutlery on plates as they ate dinner beforehand. And Beatrice, younger, far less wise, dreading Florian discovering them at any moment, knowing that what she was doing was wrong. Knowing that she was betraying her husband, knowing that she was betraying herself, and all for the sake of one night with a man who didn't love her, one man who could change her life.

Beatrice had wanted a lifetime in the theatre, and this man could get it for her. Now, sitting in the greasy cafe, Beatrice closed her eyes and tried to shut the lid of the box. But it was stuck, the lid wide open, and she could still summon up the smell of that night – flowers and claret and wood polish and him.

Her companion sighed in satisfaction. 'Ah, I see you remember Jamie Byngham perfectly well, Beatrice.'

Still Beatrice didn't speak. How on earth had this person found out what Beatrice had done? The choice she had made? Beatrice herself had practically forgotten that night – she had no idea how anyone else would have dredged it up from the annals of history. Not even Beatrice's biographer had managed to work it out.

The voice opposite her persisted. 'But do you remember what happened next, Beatrice?'

Beatrice could hear a rushing sound in her ears. She didn't hold with this modern way of diving into things that were uncomfortable. She didn't want to examine her feelings or open up or share her trauma.

'No? Well, let me remind you.'

'No. No thank you.'

'Ahhh, so you do remember. And you understand that information like that could be quite interesting to the press. Might tarnish your perfect image, don't you think?' The smile was revoltingly smug. 'So, I'd suggest that you just sign this document for me, right now, and we're all done. I won't breathe a word, and you won't be humiliated in the papers. How does that sound?'

'Like a fantasy.' Beatrice wrestled the memory box shut. There was no proof. So she had no problem. She had spent enough time with this fool. She had a show to direct, a starring role to play and a plan to enact. She rose to her feet.

'Not so fast, Beatrice.'

But she wasn't going to listen. This person had no proof of anything – they were just guessing, like everyone else always did because Beatrice never gave anything away. She had nothing to worry about, not really. She didn't need to wait any longer. It was time for actions, not words. The clock was ticking here. She would move to Plan B. She stood up and opened her purse, pulling out an envelope and thrusting it across the table. 'Here. For you. To make this go away for good.'

'Oh, Beatrice. You shouldn't have.' Fingers grabbed the envelope and tugged open the flap. 'Oh, how sweet, you actually think you can pay me off?' The voice became sugary. Honeyed. 'How very quaint. You really are a lady, aren't you?' The envelope was pushed back across the table towards Beatrice. 'But I don't want money. I have more than enough of that. No...' A long sigh. 'I want you to sign this document.' Those eyes were raking Beatrice's face again. 'Now. Or I tell the world what you did.'

Beatrice froze, wondering what to do. Here wasn't really the place to get the pistol out, but she could wait around the corner and get in a shot, just to buy herself some time – enough time to make her plan happen. But she didn't want to end up in a police cell when she could be onstage in the spotlight. She could almost hear the applause now, the adoration of the audience, her oxygen, her home. She needed her final show, her moment of glory. To go out on a high. To be Beatrice Butler, theatrical goddess, just one more time. Reluctantly, she sat back down.

'I thought you'd see sense.' The person leant towards her over the table. 'Let's see what you can do for me, Beatrice. Let's see how you can help me, for a change. You've made my life very difficult these past few weeks. A lot of people aren't happy with me, because of you. So here it is.' They pushed a familiar wad of papers across the table towards her. 'All you need to do is sign.'

Beatrice felt rage start to burn inside her. She would not be treated like this. She would come back stronger. And she knew just who she had to turn to. Someone way more powerful than this fool in front of her. Someone who had always been there for Beatrice, right from their time together in primary school. Daniel Davison had stolen Beatrice's pencil case and there her new friend had been, punching him in the face. She had helped when Florian had got sick and she would help now. Beatrice should have thought of it before.

'I know your secret, Beatrice. Don't be stupid enough to try to avoid signing this.' A pink piece of paper was pushed towards her. 'Have a read of this. See if it changes your mind. I have proof, see? Proof of what you did.'

'You had one of these delivered to me yesterday and I threw it away.' Beatrice pushed it back, refusing to look. She was damned if she was going to read it in front of this devil. What they were saying wasn't true – wasn't even close to true. She got to her feet, throwing her coat around her shoulders. She knew how to hurt this individual, and nothing was going to stop her exacting her revenge for this harassment.

'Leaving now would be a mistake. There will be consequences.' The paper was held out towards her again. She did not want it, but then her companion jumped up and stuffed it into her pocket before she could stop them.

She wasn't going to get into a scuffle, so she just let it go. She would throw the thing away later.

'I wouldn't leave if I were you, Beatrice.'

'Well, I am delighted to say that I am not you.' Beatrice swept out of the cafe, as she had done a thousand times on stage. She knew how to make an exit. And she knew how to get her revenge.

Beatrice Butler never stayed down for long. She knew exactly what she had to do. She could never let her secret come out, because the damage would diminish everything she had achieved in her long career. And there was no way on earth she would ever sign that document. She stroked the pistol through the soft leather of her bag. You didn't get to the summit of the British theatrical world by playing nice. You got there by fighting tooth and nail, by knowing your own worth, by standing up for yourself, by doing what you had to do.

If her companion wanted to play dirty, then she, Beatrice Butler, would play dirtier. She had powerful allies, and she was about to get them to wage war on her behalf. And, if that failed, then she would take aim and fire, and there was no way in hell she would ever miss.

10

JEANIE

Somebody was screaming, and Jeanie only realised it was her when a woman sitting just along the row asked nervously if Jeanie had found another dead body down there. Jeanie closed her mouth rapidly, trying to get her breath to slow down. It had just been some old tomato ketchup that her hand had brushed against – not blood. Everything was okay. Nothing to see here.

Her head was stuck under the seat, and she was searching frantically for Yumi's precious blue Jellycat bunny, which had cost nearly as much as Jeanie's entire wardrobe this evening. 'Bunny' as he was imaginatively known, was permanently being left on swings or seats, only to be dramatically missed approximately two minutes after Yumi had got off the relevant bus or finally been persuaded to leave the playground.

Jeanie extracted her head, sneezing as the dust tickled her nostrils. She looked up at the lady who had questioned her, who had long white hair and was clearly starting to panic. She put a hand to her chest. 'Is it another dead body down there? Oh my God, it is, isn't it?'

'No.' Jeanie shook her head. 'No. I'm so sorry for screaming. There are no bodies down here. I'm so sorry for worrying you.'

'Oh, thank goodness.' The woman drew an inhaler from her bag and took a sharp staccato puff. 'I don't know how much more of all this I can take. I didn't even want to come here this evening. I just wanted to stay in and watch *Antiques Roadshow*.'

'I wish we had.' The man next to her shuddered. 'Without Beatrice Butler the show will be terrible. And what if she was murdered? What if the killer comes for the rest of us?'

Jeanie straightened up, resting her hands on her knees. Wherever Yumi's bunny was, it wasn't under those seats. 'Try not to worry. We don't know that she was killed. And even if she was, it's pretty unlikely that the killer would come back for anyone else. Killers rarely want to kill people they don't know. Only assassins or terrorists do that. You know, mass murderers, that kind of thing.'

She saw from the woman's face that this line of argument wasn't helping. Stopping herself, Jeanie tried to lever herself out from the narrow space between the seats, only to discover to her embarrassment that the Christmas decorations sewn into her evil Christmas jumper appeared to have got stuck to the back of the seat in front. She tried to move upwards. No. She tried to move back down. Nothing doing. She felt like crying. She was trapped, and she very much doubted that her children were going to wait around for her to work out how to get herself free. Yumi and Jack had many talents: throwing food on the floor, giving squishy cuddles that always ended with Jeanie getting banana all over her jeans, and waking up so regularly in the night that she now felt about two hundred years old. But staying still definitely wasn't on that list, particularly when they sensed weakness. And Jeanie was well and truly stuck.

Jeanie took a deep breath to steady herself but only succeeded in inhaling a lot of dust. She tried to move one of her feet, but that was now wedged underneath the seat in front. She dug a hand around, trying to release herself, but only succeeded in grabbing a random ball of paper. She went to throw it out, before seeing the name *Beatrice Butler* in a flowing hand at the top. She wanted to read it, but the position she was in, bent double, made that process a little tricky.

Her phone vibrated in her pocket and she had to perform some serious acrobatics to get hold of it. Clio's message made her pulse rise even higher:

> BB definitely murdered. Gunshot to the head from a silver pistol. Watch what the audience do for clues.

Jeanie absorbed this. She needed to get out from down here. She jerked her foot suddenly out of its position, scraping some skin off her ankle as she did so. She then wrestled violently with her own jumper for a pointless minute or two, before beginning the laborious process of exiting the sweaty viscose. It was tough going, given that she was wedged in between two rows of seats, but she got there in the end, emerging flushed and victorious only to realise that her bra was hanging out of her ancient T-shirt and that both her children were gone.

'My kids.' She looked around. 'Did you see where they went? Anyone? My kids?'

The lady with the inhaler nodded, eyeing Jeanie a little warily, as if she was a bomb about to go off. 'The little girl looked like she needed the loo, so the little boy took her. Such a sweet pair, aren't they? Takes me right back to my childhood, going to Girl Guides, making cakes, walking my little sister to school.'

Talking too much, thought Jeanie grimly.

'But I was just down here.' She couldn't help her voice rising. 'You should have told me. They shouldn't go off on their own. They're not even three! And someone's just died. And...' She checked herself. Best not to tell everyone in here that Beatrice Butler was definitely murdered. 'If there is a killer, then they might...'

The lady twirled a long grey strand of hair. 'But you just told us that killers don't generally strike twice.'

Jeanie felt impatience surge inside her. 'I said they don't *normally* strike twice. Not that they definitely wouldn't.'

'Oh God. So we're all in danger?' The inhaler was out again and the woman took a panicky gasp.

Jeanie looked around wildly. Her twins were nowhere to be seen. 'I can't believe you just let them disappear like that.'

The woman removed the inhaler from her mouth. 'As I made perfectly clear, the girl was saying "pee pee." So please don't go blaming me for your inadequate parenting, if you please.'

Jeanie didn't have time to argue. She stood up and started scanning the theatre for the two little heads of dark hair, finding nothing except an increasingly restless audience. Small children cried, a bus party of pensioners fanned themselves with programmes, and a group with bright pink '*He's behind you*' T-shirts on were pulling flasks out of their bags and swigging regularly.

Jeanie felt panic rise inside her. She hoped the twins were still together. She hoped they would be okay. She hoped that soon they could all go home, and she could eat toast on the sofa while watching reality TV like a normal person. She hoped the killer would walk in and confess and that the twins would come back meekly from the toilets and never leave Jeanie's side again. She didn't want another murder case. She didn't want to find out who killed Beatrice Butler. She would trade everything to have her children back at her side.

She looked down absently at the pink piece of paper she had picked up from the floor, before starting to scan the theatre again. Then she looked again. A long number and a place name that she didn't recognise were scribbled on the paper, beneath Beatrice's name. Absently, she tucked it away in her pocket.

She still couldn't see her children. 'What am I going to do?'

'What do you mean, what are you going to do?' Inhaler lady was on her feet. 'What is it now?' She wrung her hands together. 'I knew I should have stayed at home. I didn't even want to come tonight. You made me, Michael!'

Her companion sat up indignantly. 'Why are you blaming me?'

'You bought the tickets.'

'Yes. Because you asked me to!' He appealed to Jeanie. 'How is this my fault?'

'I'm not going to get involved in this one.' Jeanie tried to smile reassuringly but was too worried about Yumi and Jack to intervene in anyone else's problems. She scanned the auditorium again. There were now police officers on the doors, but she wouldn't put it past her children to have worked out how to get past them. They were like a crack team of marines when it came to escaping.

This was a theatre and Jeanie knew that there was a maze of corridors behind the stage, full of dressing rooms, props stores, a green room, and then there were the wings themselves, to either side of the stage, the lighting gallery above, a cellar below. There must be hidden exits, a route to the band area under the stage and, if there were such things, then her kids would find them. As if that weren't scary enough, for all Jeanie knew, a killer might be waiting somewhere too, biding their time before making their escape.

'Yumi? Jack?' Out of the corner of her eye, behind one woman's enormous green and white striped hat – closer examination revealed that she was dressed from head to toe as an elf – Jeanie saw the twins, next to the front row, their two dark heads close together. She could imagine their gleeful exclamations as they looked at each other and realised that they could disappear, and her stomach lurched as she wondered if they had stolen anything on their journey beneath the seats to reach the holy grail of the stage.

The police officers were looking the wrong way and next thing she knew, both her children were climbing up the shallow steps and were on the stage itself. From there it was a short sprint to the trapdoor in the middle of the stage. Jeanie grabbed her bag and started to navigate her way towards them, apologising as she trod on bags or edged past legs. As she made it to the aisle, the electrical fire curtain began to descend, no doubt to protect the crime scene and ensure that there was no interference with the investigation into Beatrice's murder. Jeanie felt her heart constrict and started to move even faster, ignoring the tuts and protests that met her progress. She couldn't let her children be back there alone, not with a dead body and police and a potential killer on the loose.

They were by the trapdoor now. They were pulling at the handle. Surely it wouldn't open? Jeanie put her hand to her mouth as it did just that and the two of them disappeared inside. As was so often the case with motherhood, there was only one thing for it – Jeanie had no choice. She elbowed her way to the end of the row and then ran towards the stage. She had never been a sprinter, and she did not have the most supportive of bras on, but nothing was going to stop her protecting the twins from whoever had killed Beatrice. She put her head down, pumped her arms, and drove forward with all the strength that her out-of-condition legs could muster. Her red T-shirt matched her cheeks as she threw herself at the stage before the fire curtain fell. There was only a two-metre gap left when the police officer noticed her and yelled for her to stop. The audience, restless and seeking entertainment, began to slow clap Jeanie, whooping her on.

The curtain had only half a metre to go when Jeanie evaded the police officer with a surprisingly skilful netball sidestep and dove beneath the curtain in the nick of time. For a minute she lay, chest heaving, inhaling dust, seeing the huge lights hanging above her, getting used to the darkness. Then she ran across the stage, found the trapdoor and jumped into it, calling her children's names, reaching for them in the darkness. As she fell, she heard it slam shut above her.

It was as she was falling that she realised that she hadn't really thought things through. She fell for several metres, landing with a thud on a floor that felt like it was made of concrete. All her breath exited her body, and she felt a lurch of fear as she thought about the twins. Were they okay? Had they survived the drop?

Jeanie reached into her pocket for her phone and turned on the torch, emitting a yelp of relief when she saw Jack and Yumi alive, sitting together on a landing mat that she herself had missed by inches. They were bent over, looking at something shiny. Oh God. Please don't let it be somebody's vintage necklace. Please don't make Jeanie have to apologise for that, too.

'Yumi! Jack!' She leapt at them, enveloping them in her arms. It took them at least a second to start to wriggle, but it was enough for her to know that they were pleased to see her.

Then she saw what the shiny object was and saw the damage it could do. She reached out and grabbed it before the two of them could hurt themselves on its sharp silver blade. Why the hell was there a knife down here?

She was wondering what to do with it when she heard someone moving in the corner. Wherever they had landed, they were not alone. Someone else was in here too. Someone who could be the killer.

Jeanie froze as she considered her options. The three of them were in trouble. Deep, deep trouble. They were stuck in a dark room with a potential killer.

The only good news was that she had somehow ended up with a knife. She held it out in front of her, prepared to do whatever was necessary to protect her children and get out of here alive.

11

AMBER

Amber had never had any ambitions to go onstage, and the smell of this cow costume was not likely to change that situation any time soon. When she had snuck into the rehearsal room to see the costume exactly where Clio had promised, she had felt a pulse of triumph. She was confident it would be in fairly good shape: when she had seen Jaxon, one of the normal occupants, out front he had looked like a man who found time for personal hygiene. His hair had been clean, his clothes ironed, his teeth white. But after inserting herself underneath the abandoned Daisy costume, her face inside the mask, Amber found herself starting to regret this particular idea. Because whoever Sylvia, the front end of the cow, was, she had clearly eaten a large amount of garlic the night before. Amber would rather be anywhere but stuck in here.

She tried holding her breath but that only made it worse when she finally had to inhale. She wished she could reach the sanitiser spray that she always kept in her backpack, along with her latex gloves and her favourite magnifying glass, aka her 'fun night out kit' as Clio mockingly called it. But for now, she had no choice but to lie here and wait for Marco, and hope that he didn't notice she was hiding in the corner.

She had been lucky to get into this room unseen, thanks to a back entrance that Clio said was only normally used by the actors going on their smoking breaks. The costume had been lying on the floor next to a clothing rail full of princess outfits, frilly aprons and an itchy golden suit that looked like it would be used for Prince Charming's big finale at the end of the show.

As Amber lay quietly, inhaling the fumes, she wondered what had made Beatrice hire Dexter, and whether the two of them had clashed once they were working together again. Yes, they had been colleagues once, but what had made them decide to do so again now? Might Dexter have wanted something from Beatrice – and might he have killed her to get it? Could he have been the one to write 'Your time is over, bitch' on the dressing room mirror? Her mind raced back to the crime scene, searching for clues. What on earth was going on with the weeping Gawain? If Beatrice was so horrible to him, why did he seem so grief-stricken?

Lots of things weren't adding up, and, as Amber waited impatiently inside the cow costume, she was determined to find out how it all fitted together. But as time ticked by, she began to question whether Clio had been right about the room in which the interviews would be held. By now, if Marco had any kind of nous at all, he would have separated all the cast members and the backstage team, so that they couldn't confer and get their stories straight, potentially protecting each other and covering up what had happened. That way, he could ask difficult questions in his interviews and start to hone in on his suspects list.

However, Amber wasn't at all convinced that Marco knew what he was doing, particularly as the Bad Girls had beaten him to the killer on every case they'd ever worked in parallel. Which reminded her... She pulled her phone out of the pocket of her jeans and the screen lit up. She sent a text to one of the agency's key associates, who also happened to have recorded the voice of Giant Blunderbuss for this production. Marg Redfearn, queen of the local drugs scene, had been a very good friend of Beatrice's, if Amber's memory served her right. She was also an occasional friend to the agency, in a mutual backscratching kind of a way, and, as a result, was likely to want to help Amber to find Beatrice's killer, in return for a favour or two of course.

The text had just sent when Amber finally heard footsteps approaching and the booming voice that DI Marco Santini used when he believed he was on the trail of a killer. Amber wiggled her aching hip for the last time, grateful that Clio had been correct after all. She wondered who he would bring in first, and hoped that Clio's planned distraction would mean that he wouldn't sweep this room thoroughly, as would normally be due process in any police interview situation. She gave her nose one final scratch and tried to make herself even smaller. The costume was under a table in the corner, so fingers crossed she would not be noticed.

She heard the door open and swift footsteps approached. She heard someone whistling 'Sweet Child O' Mine' under their breath and knew that DI Marco Santini was in the room. Guns N' Roses had been his favourite band when he was growing up. The footsteps got closer and closer, and were nearly upon her, when she heard Clio's voice.

'Oh. Marco. Can I maybe listen in on the interviews, do you think?'

Marco exhaled through his nostrils with that irritating whistle he always had. It had driven Amber crazy when she had shared an incident room with him, even without his tendency to pretend that all her breakthrough ideas were his own.

'Clio.' His voice slowed to a speed so patronising you would think that Clio was a primary school kid with pigtails. 'Now, you know we can't allow that. Only police officers are allowed into the interrogation room. Only real detectives in here.'

Amber could imagine him wagging his finger in mock-recrimination. Amber felt her fists clench as they had a thousand times when they were working together. As usual, he was talking rubbish. Real detectives didn't necessarily wear a uniform. Real detectives were everywhere – true crime fans finding the solution to cases so cold they had been totally forgotten; or Clio or Jeanie, spending their time trawling through social media posts or emails, following the trail, collating evidence, finding their way to the truth. Marco thought he was a detective because he had a fancy job title and a large pay cheque, but in reality, he was just a man who asked other people to do things that he didn't fully understand himself.

'But Marco.' Amber stiffened. Clio was doing her seductive voice, roughly half an octave lower than normal and reeking of candles and late-night martinis. Amber knew it was her friend's default distraction technique around men, one honed over years of dating, that really had only ever culminated in Clio marrying a man with a bad leather jacket and a vague ability to play guitar. Her marriage to Gary had been a total disaster, as he stole Clio's money, then her home, then her daughter's savings too before leaving Clio for a cliché on legs.

Using the voice on Marco was risky, because Amber feared it would lead somewhere even worse – as Marco would have absolutely no idea that Clio was faking her flirtation. With Marco and his non-existent radar, Clio's approach might actually work. Amber knew he was looking for love. When she bumped into old colleagues around town, they always seemed to mention how their boss was on the dating apps, and how very clueless he was. Apparently, he had once ended up on a date with a seventy-year-old because he hadn't set his filters properly, and her profile picture was 'deceptively young'.

Clio carried on. 'Marco, come on. It's only me. No one would ever know. And it wouldn't be for the agency, no way. I'm just an interested amateur.' Amber heard her friend's footsteps moving across the floor towards the cow costume. Marco was only a couple of metres away from where Amber lay. She held her breath. 'Oh, look, it's some mistletoe. Just above your head.' Clio gave a tiny laugh as Amber cringed inside Daisy.

Clio continued. 'You and I could be – I don't know – the Mistletoe Murder Club! Go on. I could just hide in the cupboard over there. I'm only tiny.' The footsteps turned and walked back towards where the table had been. Amber could imagine her friend giving Marco her widest eyes. Amber wondered whether the green make-up ruined the effect.

Marco swallowed audibly. 'Well, now, I don't know...'

Clio's voice got even more husky. 'And let's face it, I'm really good at solving murders.'

Amber winced. That was exactly what *not* to say to Detective Inspector Marco Santini. He was already angry with the Bad Girls for all the good press they had gained from solving several murder cases before the police. Reminding him of how effective Amber, Jeanie and Clio were as a detective team was not going to help matters now.

When he replied, his voice was icy. 'Clio, enough chatting. I must ask you to leave the room. I am setting up for preliminary interviews, which are about to begin, and one of which will be with you as a cast member who was heard by a witness saying that she would like to kill Beatrice Butler earlier tonight.'

Amber winced. No, Clio. Not again. Nearly two years ago Clio had been prime suspect in Gary's murder and had spent a night in a holding cell.

'What?' Clio laughed. 'That wasn't a serious threat, Marco. You know me. I...'

'Out. Now.' Amber could hear him shepherding Clio to the door. 'I will speak to you in due course.'

The door closed as Amber digested what she had heard. Obviously, Marco had already had police officers doing preliminary fact-finding interviews. This was speedy for Marco – which meant the press must already know the situation. He was trying to stay ahead of the game and catch the killer fast. Marco loved nothing more than a 'good news, aren't we brilliant?' news conference. Any untimely death was big news for Sunshine Sands, where headlines were normally about a reduction in bin collections or a local car boot sale making record takings. But the death of a celebrity would go national, and whatever her apparent faults, Beatrice Butler was most definitely a celebrity. Old people knew her from her TV heyday in *Top Deck*, while younger people knew her from her appearances on a popular YouTube channel, playing a disturbingly familiar role of 'grumpy old woman'. Her death might make Sunshine Sands go global for all the wrong reasons, so Marco was probably being given every resource under the sun to bring this case home.

He was whistling again, and Amber lay there on the vinyl floor, gritting her teeth. Clio's decoy had worked – he didn't approach her again. She heard a table being dragged towards the window, and imagined him throwing his digital recorder, his paperwork and his notebook and pens on the table. His lack of organisation had driven her mad when he had been her boss. His notes were chaotic, and the questions he posed were sometimes complete non-sequiturs, aggravating both witnesses and their lawyers. In addition, Marco always had a suspects board, where he fixated on one option, generally linked to drugs in some way, and missed the real killer until Amber and the team led him there kicking and screaming. And now he was the one in the top job, while Amber was lying underneath a smelly pantomime cow. Where was the justice in that?

Amber felt hunger gnawing inside her when someone else entered the room, their light footsteps tapping across the floor. Amber didn't dare to peek out from underneath the costume, but she believed that it must be a woman out there, settling into the seat opposite Marco.

Marco coughed and began.

'Please could you state your name for the tape.'

'Kylie Silver.'

Amber nodded to herself as Kylie kept talking. 'I'm playing the lead role, Jack.' Amber remembered what Clio had said on the Bad Girls WhatsApp group about Kylie. Apparently, she was sweet, young, good at doing her nails, and, somewhat incredibly, in love with Dexter Buchanan.

Marco spoke again. 'So, Kylie, tell me where you were during the last half-hour before the curtain was due to go up.'

Kylie spoke clearly, as if this was some kind of audition tape for a role that would provide her big break. 'Well, I was doing my, like, make-up?' She seemed to talk in questions. 'In Dexter's dressing room?' She gave a tinkling giggle that set Amber's teeth on edge. 'He and I are… together, you know, right?'

Oh, dear lord. This was going to be a long one. Amber hoped her tummy didn't start to rumble. She should have nicked some of Clio's Nutella before settling down in here.

Marco spoke. 'You and Dexter Buchanan are romantically involved?'

'Yes.' Another giggle.

'I see.'

'Anyway, we were both getting ready, you know. I was helping him with his wrinkles. To cover them up, right?'

Amber bet Dexter would love that particular revelation.

'That's all we were doing, really. Our dressing room is miles from where Beatrice was. So we didn't hear anything, really. We saw someone rushing down the corridor, maybe around seven-fifteen? But I didn't see who it was.' A pause. 'But I think it was a woman?'

'A woman rushed down the corridor at around seven-fifteen, you're saying?'

Kylie answered quickly. 'Yeah. Like, not a man.'

'Thank you for that.' Amber could hear sarcasm in Marco's voice.

'No problem. It's the little details that count, isn't it?' Kylie sounded pleased with herself. 'In those detective series on TV there's always a detail, isn't there? It's always the little things that give away who did it. Like a man wearing only one sock. Or a hair grip in the wrong place. You know? That man with the moustache…'

'Hercule Poirot?'

'That's the one. He always notices the little things, doesn't he?'

'Um. Yes. Yes, he does.' Marco sounded tired. For once, Amber didn't blame him. 'And Dexter was with you the whole time?'

'Yes. Absolutely.' Kylie giggled. 'There's no stopping him, if you know what I mean.'

Amber heard the zip of a bag opening. 'Just got to touch up my make-up.'

'I…'

'Dexter doesn't like it if I don't look my best.' Giggle. Amber was struggling not to scream.

'Dexter wanted to have – you know…?' Giggle. 'A moment. The two of us.

Before we went onstage. He said it helped him to centre himself? To get in the zone.'

That's one way of putting it, thought Amber.

'And then we heard someone screaming that Beatrice was dead, like, coming down the corridor, and we ran out and went to her dressing room. But Clio wouldn't let us in.'

'Clio?'

'Yeah. She was in there with Gawain.'

'Was she now?'

'Yeah, didn't you know that? I thought you were a detective.' Giggle. But this time, Amber smiled. Nice one, Kylie.

He sighed. 'And you didn't see anyone on the way to Beatrice's dressing room?'

'No. Maybe. I can't remember.' Giggle. Then there was a long pause. 'I was really just thinking about the show and about Dexter. You know? I love him so much.'

There was a knock on the door.

'Interview terminated at 20.15.' Marco got to his feet. 'You can go now, Miss Silver.'

'Thank you.' A chair was scraped back. 'You look dead handsome, by the way. You're quite a silver fox, aren't you?'

Amber couldn't hold it in any longer. She groaned.

Footsteps came towards her and the costume was wrenched off. Amber got the irrational urge to cover herself, as if she was naked.

'Oh my God!' Kylie's hand flew to her mouth. 'A spy!'

Marco's eyes glinted. 'Miss Silver. You can go. I'll deal with this.'

The girl scurried out, glancing back at Amber over her shoulder.

Marco folded his arms, staring down at Amber, who felt like she was frozen into her prone position. She moved a leg and heard a loud click.

He sighed. 'Amber Nagra. I should have known you'd be mixed up in all this. Trust you and bloody Clio. Mistletoe Murder Club, indeed. Get out of here before I sue you for illegal trespass, eavesdropping and wasting police time.'

Amber tried to stand up, but discovered that it was harder than it should be. She pushed up on her hand and managed to make it to all fours. She took a breath and attempted to make it to standing, only to hit her head on the table.

'Ow.'

'Get out.' He turned away. But Amber had to try to see if she could find anything out. She staggered to her feet and peered sideways, trying to scan the files and papers that were on the table, just in case she could see anything, something that might make a difference.

She looked up to find him staring at her, a frown biting between his brows.

'Amber. I know what you're up to. Go. Get out. Leave. Now. Before I have to arrest you.'

Amber held her hands up and ran out to find Jeanie.

12

CLIO

After her eviction from the rehearsal room, Clio had been sent by a determinedly grumpy police officer to the pungent dressing room next door. She was waiting, aka looking around for clues, when she heard Amber being kicked out. 'Damn.' Clio paced the tiny room, wishing Amber had been able to stay in to overhear more interviews and wondering what her friend had picked up in terms of clues.

Clio could hear Amber being walked back along to the main auditorium, where she would probably be penned back in with the rest of the audience for what would probably prove to be a very long time. She was wondering when she would be called through for questioning when she heard a door squeak in the room on the other side of hers and then the sound of a phone ringing. She pressed her ear to the wall, listening hard, looking around for a glass to press to the decaying green wallpaper. Forget privacy – everything was fair game at this stage of an investigation. She grabbed an unwashed tumbler, positioning it in front of an indentation in the wallpaper. She pressed her ear to the glass and listened in.

'I did it!' The voice was jubilant. 'I bloody did it!'

This comment was met with silence, so presumably whoever it was must be on the other end of the line. Clio leant closer. It sounded like Ross. But what would be crowing about? Had he sold a house? Had he tracked down a piece of Shirley Temple memorabilia to feed his growing collection, or something? Her mind tangled on how different he sounded – his cheerful tones in marked contrast to his obvious grief when they had spoken earlier. Now, he sounded like he had just arrived at a party with a glass of fizz in his hand and his eye on the canapé tray.

Filled with creeping dread, Clio remembered the strands of mistletoe she had seen on his costume earlier – and the strands that had been wrapped around the barrel of the gun that had killed Beatrice.

She listened even more intently as he carried on.

'Yes! I know! I mean, I did promise you I'd get it done.' He gave a low bubbling laugh. It was definitely Ross. She had heard that laugh many times, on every night they'd had one too many margaritas at The Ovation after a rehearsal or a show. She loved that laugh and she was very fond of the man it belonged to, considered him to be her friend.

'So now there's nothing standing in our way.' This time there was a triumphant note. 'Full steam ahead.'

There was a pause and Clio pressed herself so close to the wall she was in danger of impaling herself on a prominent picture hook.

Ross's voice had dropped even lower. 'She's out of the picture.'

Clio's ear was starting to ache but there was no way she was pulling away from the wall. No way on earth. She needed to hear what Ross said next. She had too many questions. Was he essentially claiming that he'd killed Beatrice? Ross couldn't even use a tin opener – there was no way he would ever pick up a gun and fire it.

Unless Clio was wrong about him. She had form – she'd been very, very wrong about her ex, Gary. Now, in the stuffy dressing room, she searched for reasons, searched for excuses for her friend. Maybe he wasn't talking about Beatrice – but Clio didn't believe in coincidences that big. Or maybe this wasn't Ross – maybe it was the real killer pretending to be Ross to put Clio off the scent. Maybe this conversation had been set up somehow, maybe the killer was trying to trick her.

Her mind whirred through the suspects list as she waited to hear more. The list was long. There was Winnie, the put-upon stage manager, though frankly she didn't appear to have the gumption to brush her own hair, let alone kill anyone. Then there was Gawain the set designer, but he had appeared so devastated by Beatrice's death that it appeared unlikely that he was the culprit. And what about the stage light that had nearly crushed Beatrice yesterday? Surely that wasn't a coincidence? Was that the killer's first attempt to end Beatrice's life?

The silence continued on the other side of the wall. Clio considered the others: Kylie, Dexter, Sylvia, Jaxon – and the Sunshine Sizzlers, all twenty-two of them. At least they had been getting ready in the cafe on the other side of the square at the time of the murder, so presumably they could be knocked off the suspect list. And then there was Clio herself, of course. She would be interviewed soon, and no doubt Marco would find some crazy way to decide that she must have killed Beatrice. He had done it before.

The real problem with this case, Clio reflected, was that there were too many suspects. During the course of the four-week rehearsal period, Beatrice had made everyone cry at least once, and she had not confined her critiques to their performances, but had widened them to include their weight, their life choices, their hairstyles, their everything. It was as if she wanted them to hate her. Clio herself had come under fire for being wooden and for having a hair colour more interesting than she was herself.

Clio had shrugged it off, of course, and had used her traditional coping strategy of going home and having three margaritas and an entire slab of Cadbury's Caramel. But she had resented Beatrice's words, just as she had resented the vicious glee with which they were delivered. Clio had worked with sadistic directors before, but Beatrice had a coldness to her that made Clio feel like a verruca about to be lanced, rather than the trained professional actress she actually was. And she knew so many other members of the cast felt the same. Given the levels of stage fright backstage tonight, any one of them could have been pushed over the edge and taken a shot.

She heard the voice again. 'OK, so once I've got this interview out of the way I'll meet you, right? Where is it again? The pier, outside the candy store at the end? At midnight? Okay. Bye.'

Clio tucked this information away. If she could, she would be there too, and she would find out what Ross had done and what he had got mixed up in. She thought back to the contents of his rucksack earlier – the signed script. Where had he got the money for that? Unease prickled through her. Of all the members of the cast and crew, she didn't want her bestie to be the bad guy. She remained leaning against the wall, her ear to the glass, even though the voice had stopped, thinking it all through. Maybe Ross could be the killer. Maybe he was a far better actor than she had realised. He was big and bulky, maybe he had the strength to hold Beatrice down and hold a pistol to her temple.

As she was thinking this she looked down and saw a scrap of paper on the floor. She reached down and picked it up, scrunching up her eyes as she read the words. It was a betting slip, and she saw from the date and time that it was for a race that had taken place earlier in the afternoon. Clio frowned as she saw the figure on the slip. It was an astronomical amount, the kind of bet that you place when you are utterly desperate, when you need a big win just to stay on track.

She tapped the slip with her fingers, thinking. Everyone had been at the final dress rehearsal this afternoon, so maybe this belonged to one of the back-stage crew? To stage manager Winnie? Or set designer Gawain? Or even to Jaxon or Sylvia, who had a lengthy break from Daisy the Cow in Act Two, and who could perfectly well have popped out to the betting shop to place their money on a horse called Hoof Hearted. But where had they got the money from? There had been a lot of thefts recently. Could the killer have shot Beatrice in order to pay their gambling debts? She wondered if Hoof Hearted had romped home, or if the horse had fallen at the first fence. Maybe the latter was what had triggered the murder – maybe the killer had tried to scare Beatrice into handing over the ring, but then shot her when she refused.

Clio inhaled deeply. Perhaps it hadn't been Ross who had killed Beatrice. Maybe the clues would lead to someone else. She felt a beat of hope, making a plan as she stood there, still in her hessian sack and green body paint. She needed to find Amber and Jeanie and talk this through. She had to go to the Sunshine Sands betting shop and find out who had laid this bet. And then the three of them would go to the pier at midnight, to see what Ross was up to. Yes. She took a deep breath. These were the next steps in what was clearly going to be a complicated investigation.

She pulled her phone out and took a picture of the slip. Just as she had done so, she heard a knock on the door and dropped it back to the floor, so that she couldn't be accused of impeding the investigation. Then, she went outside to be interviewed by DI Marco Santini about whether she was the one who had murdered Beatrice Butler.

13

JEANIE

From her position under the stage, Jeanie could hear footsteps above her. Loud footsteps, and then some kind of strange sweeping sound that made her wonder if someone was trying to clear the stage of some form of evidence. She didn't have time to worry about that, however – her main priority was to protect her twins from whoever was down here with them.

When she had followed her twins through the trapdoor, Jeanie had been more worried about them hurting themselves than about them actually encountering the killer. But now that she was down here, in the dark, brandishing a dagger in her shaking hand, she realised how foolish she had been. What kind of mum was she, letting the two of them come down here? Why hadn't she kept them at home where they were safe, where mad killers couldn't get to them? Jeanie should have known that any attempt at a night out for the three Bad Girls detectives would inevitably lead to murder. The children ought to be tucked up in bed, not stuck down here with a potential killer. Frankly, if they survived this, the twins would be very lucky to ever leave the house again.

Not that Yumi and Jack seemed remotely bothered by the situation. Jeanie had dived in front of them when she realised they had company, switching off her phone torch, so that the killer wouldn't be able to aim in their direction, but she could hear them giggling merrily behind her, clearly thinking that this whole adventure was a huge joke.

'Snack, Mama?'

There was a loud scrape from the far corner of wherever they were – a cellar? – where the stranger must be watching them, assessing what to do next.

Jeanie half-turned towards the twins. 'Ssssssh.'

But Yumi was not one to be shushed. 'Snack. Now.'

'Later.'

'Mamaaa.' Their whines were challenging even at home, but down here they were overwhelming. Jeanie inhaled deeply and got a noseful of dust for her trouble. She heard more scraping and wondered if whoever was here with them was dragging out some kind of weapon. Oh God. Her pulse spiralled and she moved forwards, aiming the dagger towards the corner. She would protect her babies. She would go down fighting. She would never say die. She raised her voice, proud when it came out steady and true.

'Whoever you are, stop right there. I have a dagger and I'm not afraid to use it.'

The scraping stopped and by some miracle the twins kept quiet too. Maybe Jeanie should use a desperate dagger voice with them more often.

She felt her hand start to shake. She had last held a weapon during a 'relaxing' weekend away back in February, when she, Amber and Clio ended up trying to catch a killer in an isolated castle. She had hated it then too – the sense that she could kill someone simply by using the item she was holding. She didn't want to be capable of murder. She didn't want that kind of power, could never imagine deciding to end someone else's existence. But now her kids were under threat, and she had no choice but to keep them safe however she could.

She spoke again, with all the authority she could muster. 'Whoever you are, switch on the light.'

A scrabble, then silence. For a moment, Jeanie was afraid that there was some secret exit, and that whoever this was would disappear through it and lock them in for ever. Then, suddenly, light flooded the cellar. Jeanie blinked in the sudden glare, checking behind her to see that her children were all right. They were, with Jack lunging for a set of colourful juggling balls that were lying next to the crumbling wall behind them and Yumi transfixed by a sparkly tiara on a set of shelves to her left. This basement room, with its low vaulted ceilings, was a treasure trove, full of costumes, bits of scenery and props. It would be quite an achievement if she ever got the twins to leave.

Jeanie turned her attention back to their companion, seeing a bedraggled woman with long, dark hair and a severe fringe. She had seen the face before, somewhere. Where had it been? She was holding up shaking hands, her face turned away from Jeanie, as if she truly believed that Jeanie was about to stab her. Her shoulders heaved and tears were rolling down her face.

Jeanie couldn't afford to relent just yet. Not until she knew more. 'What's your name?'

The woman struggled for breath. 'Winnie.'

'And what are you doing down here?'

Winnie's voice sounded thick, dry, like she needed a drink. 'Gawain – the set designer – told me at around seven o'clock that the trapdoor wasn't working in rehearsal earlier, and he didn't have time to have a look, he said.' She was talking so fast that her words were running into each other, her fingers playing with the silver Christmas tree motif on her top. 'Beatrice kept getting stuck halfway up when she was making her entrance, and of course, it needed to be sorted before tonight. So I came straight down to have a go at figuring it out, if I could. I'm the stage manager, you see. And Beatrice's assistant. Normally, I'd have been with Beatrice, making sure she had everything she needed, but this was more important. And I fixed the trapdoor – but it shut when I was down here and the controls are up there... Your kids must have set them off or something to get down here.' She pointed up towards the stage. 'And the door through to the rest of the backstage area was locked, and now I can't get out.' She wiped her nose with her sleeve, giving a huge sniff. Then she blinked in evident surprise. 'Um. I think your son is about to...'

Jeanie turned round to see Jack leaning forwards to pick up an axe. For such a young child, he had a terrifying attraction to lethal objects. Jeanie quickly grabbed a set of plastic plates and cups from the shelves and placed them in front of him, removing the axe and placing it to her right. 'Here. Play with these for a bit. Let's have a tea party.'

Yumi's eyes lit up at the sight of the cups and she moved towards them. Jeanie predicted that she had about one minute till they started fighting over them. She looked up, weighing her words carefully. If Winnie had been trapped down here when the murder happened, then it was possible that she would have absolutely no idea that Beatrice was dead.

'Winnie. We don't have long so I'm not going to mess around. Do you know why the trapdoor wasn't working?'

Winnie shrugged. 'Someone had jammed the mechanism. I just found this...' She held out a long spanner. 'This was stuck into the cogs that move the trapdoor upwards.'

'Which actors use the trapdoor?'

'Just Dexter and Beatrice, really.'

Jeanie's mind raced. 'And the trapdoor is only for entrances and exits, I guess?'

Winnie nodded. 'Yes.'

'So why would someone jam it? So Dexter and Beatrice couldn't get on or offstage?'

Winnie shrugged. 'I don't know why anyone would do that, to be honest. But yeah – maybe, to stop them getting onstage. Especially with the locked door too.' Her brow furrowed. 'Why are you asking these questions?'

Jeanie watched Winnie carefully. This was Jeanie's style of detecting: she asked questions, she listened and she observed. Clio was more about the spontaneous impulse side of things, going for mad hunches, making up random theories, while Amber missed nothing. Ever. She was forensic in her analysis, and kept piecing layers of a case together until she had solved it. They were the dream team, or so Jeanie thought, anyway.

A big tear rolled down Winnie's cheek. 'Beatrice is going to kill me. She hates it when I'm not where I'm meant to be. She's going to think I let her down, she's going to yell at me, or think that I hid down here to get out of doing my job.'

Jeanie felt a rush of sympathy. She would have to tell Winnie about Beatrice. She really didn't want to be the one to do it, but it seemed unkind to let her believe that everything was okay. Jeanie inhaled, preparing to speak.

Winnie was still talking though, her eyes scared. 'She can be so mean, Beatrice. I didn't really want to work for her, but she made me. She reads me like a book, you see. Ever since I started working for her, she just knew what I was thinking, all of the time. It was scary, to be honest, like she was tapping my phone or something. And then she used those things to make me do what she wanted.'

Behind her, Jeanie sensed the twins about to escalate. 'Things like what?'

'Well.' Winnie put her head on one side. 'Things like...' She hesitated. 'She made me stir things up within the cast, like making Jaxon think that Sylvia was seeing someone else behind his back.'

Jeanie blinked. 'I beg your pardon?'

'Oh yes.' Winnie nodded. 'Beatrice thinks that a bit of creative tension amongst members of the cast is healthy, that it—' her fingers made air quotes '—creates an amazing artistic dynamic that leads to great productions.' She shrugged. 'That's a direct quote. And once she found out more about me, about my family, the mistakes I've made, she just took advantage.'

Jeanie nodded. 'I see.'

Winnie fiddled with the laces on her trainers. 'Beatrice is a great director, mind. She knows what she's doing. And she won't ever change, not for anyone.' She twirled her hair around and around in her hand so fast that it looked like a helicopter blade before take-off.

'Breaking up Jaxon and Sylvia was just one in a long line of bad things she made me do. Things that hurt people.' Her mouth twisted. 'But there's something about her – it's so hard to say no. There's a reason that she's the nation's darling. She's just so charismatic. And as her assistant I get a lot of perks – invites to shows, that kind of thing, as long as I keep my side of the bargain and keep things moving the way she wants them to.'

A shout came from behind Jeanie. 'MINE.' Jack's voice was so loud that Jeanie nearly had a cardiac arrest.

'NO, MINE.' Yumi matched his volume with an impressive shriek of her own.

'MINE!'

Jeanie sighed inwardly. There was only one way this argument was going to go.

'So, Winnie, do you mean that Beatrice has basically been manipulating this cast the whole time?'

Winnie narrowed her eyes. 'Hang on. Why are you asking so many questions about Beatrice?' She put her hand to her mouth. 'Oh God, you're not press, are you? She'll kill me.'

'No.' Jeanie shook her head. 'I'm not press, don't worry. But...'

Behind her, the children's squabbling increased. Jeanie reached a hand back, ineffectually grabbing for them. No small hands were to be found, but at least they were still there, in the room, where she could protect them.

'But what?' Winnie leant forward, eyes bright. 'What's happened? You're scaring me.'

'Um—' Jeanie didn't know how to say it.

'Yes?' Winnie watched her, eyes wide.

Jeanie wondered if Winnie was faking the fear in her eyes. Maybe she already knew what had happened to Beatrice, maybe she had run away down here after killing her, cleverly setting up her own alibi. Jeanie observed her, the long fingers frantically weaving in and out of her hair, the way that she was chewing on her lower lip. If she was a killer, then she was very good at hiding it.

Jeanie took a deep breath. 'I'm afraid that Beatrice is dead.'

Winnie froze, colour draining from her cheeks like water let out of a bath. 'What?'

A plastic plate flew past Jeanie's face, landing with a thud against the floor. A mug followed, then some plastic cutlery. Jeanie winced. The twins were going nuclear, but Jeanie kept her eyes on Winnie's face. 'Beatrice is dead. She's been murdered – shot in the head backstage, in her dressing room.'

Winnie blinked. 'Who on earth would murder Beatrice?'

'We don't know yet.' Jeanie chose her words carefully. 'But it does sound like maybe some people didn't like her very much?'

Winnie looked as if she had been slapped. 'Yes, but they still want to work with her. She's such a legend. A theatrical pioneer, a national treasure, a visionary.' Winnie could be reading from the pages of Beatrice's biography. Then her face changed and she put her hand to her mouth. 'Was, I mean.' Her face crumpled and she pressed the heels of her hands to her eyes. 'Oh God. I can't believe this. I can't believe she's gone. What will I do now?' Winnie let the tears roll down her face, seemingly unaware that they were there. They dripped off her chin onto her top. 'I didn't know she would go so soon.'

This struck a strange note. Go so soon? What did she mean? Beatrice was well over seventy, but in robust health, from what Clio had said. Jeanie wanted to find out more. 'I'm so sorry, Winnie. It must be so hard.' Another plate flew past Jeanie's ear. 'How long had you worked for her?'

'A couple of years.' Winnie sniffed. 'I started with her just after she'd won the Olivier award for her Medea at the National. Did you see it?'

No, Jeanie had not. Jeanie had been deep in the IVF trenches at that point. 'No, but I bet it was amazing.' She had to get the children to quieten down, just for a little bit longer. Jeanie reached into her bag, finding a long-forgotten roll of Fruit Pastilles. She grabbed them with eager fingers and gave them to the twins, who fell on them like wolves on a deer carcass. Late night plus sweets – Jeanie would need a flak jacket to get through the day tomorrow.

'It was amazing.' Winnie's eyes were dreamy now. 'Someone sent me a ticket, so I went along. She was so powerful up there. Yet so fragile. Such a stunning performance. I went to the stage door afterwards and got her autograph, and I think her old assistant had just left or something and she wanted to hire me. I couldn't believe it.' There was a bitter twist to her mouth that somehow didn't match her words. Jeanie's curiosity was growing.

'And did you ever want to act too?'

Winnie shook her head quickly, not quite meeting Jeanie's eye. 'Oh no. I have no acting talent at all. I just wanted to be a part of this world, you know? The world of theatre, a world where you can make anything come true with some lights and a stage and a decent script. I mean, I know it doesn't look the most glamorous life right now...' She almost smiled as she looked around at the dusty cellar. 'But I love being her right-hand woman, seeing the posters go up, the tickets being sold, and knowing that I played a tiny part in it all.'

Jeanie heard paper ripping behind her and knew that the sweets would run out all too soon.

Winnie was twirling her hair again. 'I can't believe anyone would want to kill her. Not really.'

Jeanie nodded. 'Well...'

Winnie shook her head. 'I just – I mean, she was... She was just Beatrice, you know?'

'But how did it make you feel? When she was unkind? Did you ever get angry?'

Winnie's big brown eyes glinted. 'Angry? No.'

'Why not?'

Winnie shrugged. 'Well, recently she's been a bit more – extreme than usual. A bit meaner, I suppose. But I forgave her because I knew what she was going through.'

'And what was that?'

'Um.' Winnie opened her mouth and closed it again. 'Well, I guess I can tell you now. Beatrice wanted me to keep it a secret.'

'Tell me what?'

Winnie pressed her lips together. 'That Beatrice Butler was dying.'

Jeanie put her head on one side. 'What? Do you mean that you knew someone was going to kill her?'

Winnie shook her head violently. 'No. God, no. Not at all. I'd have stopped them if that was the case. No, what I knew was that they needn't have bothered killing her.' She met Jeanie's eyes. 'Because she told me she only had months to live. She had cancer.'

Jeanie's mouth fell open.

'Yes.' Winnie nodded. 'She never let me tell anyone, but I arranged all her appointments. So yes – whoever killed her could simply have waited and nature would have done the work for them.' She frowned, staring at Jeanie's hand. 'Can I just ask, why do you have Beatrice's letter knife? Did you bring it down here with you?'

Jeanie looked down, jolted when she saw the weapon in her hand. She had totally forgotten about it.

'Um. I found it. Down here. And I thought you might be the killer, so, you know, I picked it up. To defend my kids.'

Winnie frowned, really puzzled now. She peered closer. 'Why is her letter knife down here?'

'I have absolutely no idea.' Jeanie looked down at the long silver knife, engraved, now she looked at it, with the initials BB.

'Her husband gave that to her.' Winnie reached for it, but Jeanie pulled it away from her grasp. With her children in here she just couldn't take the risk, no matter how innocent Winnie appeared. Jeanie couldn't trust her. She couldn't afford to get that wrong.

'She used it every day.' Winnie smiled. 'She loved writing, keeping a record of her life. She had this gorgeous fountain pen that used real ink cartridges, and she always used thick cream paper and the same notebooks every time. She was a class act, you know? One of the old school.'

Jeanie thought to herself that it sounded like Beatrice was a proper bully too, but refrained from saying anything out loud.

Winnie kept talking. 'Her husband was always buying her gorgeous things. Like her ruby ring from Cartier. It was worth a lot of money, and she never took it off. She said Florian gave it to her on a trip to Paris.' Winnie sighed. 'It was so romantic. They fell in love as soon as they read together, in panto. *Jack and the Beanstalk*. That's why she wanted to do it again – one last time. But now she never will.' Her face fell. 'You know, I do wonder why the letter knife is down here? She always kept it in her bag.'

So did Jeanie. Could Beatrice herself have dropped it down here during one of her entrances or exits?

She was jolted by a scream from behind her. She turned. 'What is it now, you two? What?'

An empty packet lay on the floor. The sweets had run out. It was time to get out of here.

Jeanie put the knife back in her bag, ready to hand in to the police. 'Come on, Winnie. Let's get out of here. I'm sure that between us we can break down this door.' She held out her hands for the twins. 'We need to get back up to the auditorium.'

Winnie started crying again. 'I don't want to see the body. I don't think I could bear it. This is too much. I can't believe she's gone.'

Jeanie felt a rush of sympathy. 'It's okay. We'll look after you.'

'Thank you.' Winnie sniffed again, making an ineffectual dab at her cheeks. 'It just doesn't make sense though, does it?'

'What do you mean?'

'Well, why murder her today of all days? She told me earlier that she was going to tell the cast today about her illness, just after her meeting about saving the theatre.'

Jeanie stopped. 'What meeting?'

Winnie sniffed loudly. 'She had a meeting with someone today about ensuring that the theatre would never get demolished. Its future has been hanging in the balance ever since the council gave planning permission for the new social housing estate, because this theatre is right on the edge of it, where they want to put the new leisure centre. Beatrice told me there was no way she was going to die without knowing the theatre would be here for ever.' Winnie sighed. 'But I was out on errands so I'm not sure if she ever got around to it.'

Jeanie remembered Clio's harsh words earlier, when the twins had escaped backstage. It seemed unlikely that even Clio would say how much she hated someone who had just announced they had a terminal disease. So maybe Beatrice hadn't told them yet. She took Jack and Yumi by the hand and led them towards the trapdoor. Their eyes were too bright, their bodies too full of a manic energy. This was a code red parenting situation and Jeanie needed to get them home.

She stood on her tiptoes and pushed the trapdoor, but it didn't move an inch. Jeanie swallowed, nervously. 'Oh no. You were right. It's impossible to push up from underneath. It's too heavy.'

The twins were starting to cry now. Jeanie couldn't blame them. Bending low, she strode across to the locked door that Winnie had said led to the rest of the backstage area. She would just have to bust it open somehow. She wasn't staying down here a minute longer. She wanted to call Tan and tell him they were all okay. She wanted to breathe fresh air. And she wanted to tuck her kids up safely in their beds.

Nothing was going to stop her.

Jeanie took a deep breath and sprinted towards the door, slamming her body into it with all the force she could muster.

It flew open and she fell in a heap onto a drum kit, making the kind of clatter that she normally associated with the twins' sensory music class.

Once the twins had come through, Jeanie turned and looked back at the door.

The bolt was pulled back.

It hadn't been locked at all.

She looked at Winnie. Winnie looked back. Then she slunk away towards the stairs.

Jeanie didn't know what was going on, but she couldn't wait to talk to Clio and Amber. Her phone chimed. It was Clio, changing the Bad Girls WhatsApp icon to a picture of mistletoe and renaming it 'The Mistletoe Murder Club.' Jeanie gave a small smile. She had to investigate this murder alongside her friends. She had to find out why someone would kill a dead woman walking. She had to start understanding why someone had believed that Beatrice Butler needed to die tonight.

14

BEATRICE BUTLER

11.25: Eight hours until her death

'So, Beatrice, what is it you want? Do we need to re-record my lines?'

Marg Redfearn sat opposite Beatrice in the Westbury Hotel on the seafront, the two of them having a late breakfast, as they had done many times before. Marg's black reading glasses were perched on her nose as she perused the menu she must know as well as she knew the back of her hand. Beatrice knew that Marg would read through it once, and then have the continental breakfast, like she always did.

'No, nothing like that.' Even Beatrice knew better than to ask Marg to re-record anything. Despite dressing like a leading member of the local WI – all cashmere and pearls – Marg was in fact a local business legend, with a sideline in drugs trafficking. She and Beatrice had first met in the school playground and had been firm friends ever since. Marg had really come through for Beatrice when Florian had succumbed to a serious cocaine addiction, facing up to her terrifying father, and persuading him to stop supplying Florian with the drugs he craved. Initially her protestations had fallen on deaf ears, until Marg's father had realised that Beatrice had played the mermaid in his favourite TV movie *The Secrets of the Sea*. One swift journey to rehab later and Florian had discovered that his supply had been brutally cut off and the problem had never reoccurred.

Beatrice had performed a poem at Marg's second wedding as a thank you – something by Keats, as she recalled, and from then on, she and Marg had re-established their friendship. They had one rule: that they never ever talked about their work. Marg was bored out of her mind by Beatrice's stage gossip, while Beatrice would rather have plausible deniability if the police ever questioned her about her association with Marg and her various enterprises. So they talked houseplants, telly (they both adored *Ludwig*), Marg's boyfriends and their favourite topic: how Sunshine Sands was better in the old days.

Until today. Today, Beatrice needed Marg's help. Today, things were about to change.

Beatrice eyed her friend severely. 'Marg, you know perfectly well that you recorded those lines perfectly.' They both fell silent as the waiter brought their coffees in thick china cups. There were discreet golden Ws just beneath the rim and tiny silver spoons lay in the saucers. Marg asked for cream instead of milk and the waiter nodded eagerly, no doubt aware that he could not afford to anger these two particularly precious customers. Beatrice could see the manager hovering in the corner, immaculate in his dark suit, palms pressed together in something like prayer. She knew that he would be more worried about offending Marg than her, and for once she didn't mind playing second fiddle to her companion. Sometimes she liked to imagine what Marg got up to in the name of work, but generally decided to stop this line of thought when she got to the lethal weapons her friend might use.

Beatrice looked Marg straight in the eye. She had to hand it to her – Marg looked good. It must be that new young man she had in tow – the one with the tan and the muscles bulging beneath his tight blue T-shirt. Beatrice hadn't bothered to remember his name when Marg had mentioned it – she knew by now that he would be gone before the month was out. Marg never kept them long.

She folded her hands neatly in front of her. 'Marg, I need your help.'

'Oh yes?' Marg flicked an imaginary fleck of dust from her navy-blue sleeve. Beatrice smiled to herself – as if anything would dare to land on Marg Redfearn.

She swallowed, wondering how to phrase this. 'I have a little… problem.'

Marg didn't miss a beat. 'Well, tell me who it is and I'll kill them.'

Beatrice swallowed, not entirely sure if Marg was joking. 'It's not exactly that kind of problem.'

Marg put her head on one side, her short white hair falling perfectly into place, clearly unused to not simply killing problems off. 'What do you mean, Beatrice? Spit it out.'

'Well. I have a – a secret.' Beatrice swallowed nervously.

'Don't we all?' Marg arched her eyebrows as she sipped her coffee.

The two of them sat back as the waiter appeared again. Beatrice had a crisp white napkin laid across her lap and she felt like there was hope in the air as a tray of pastries was set down in front of her. With Marg's help, she could get this done. She could keep the past where it belonged and secure the theatre's future.

She took a sip of the coffee, savouring its smoky sweetness. The Westbury was the most decadent breakfast spot in town, bar none.

Marg reached for a puffy golden pain au chocolat. 'Come on then. Out with it.'

Beatrice squared her shoulders. 'I did something rather foolish, Marg. When I was young.'

'Who didn't?' Marg nodded approvingly as a toast-rack full of perfect tiny triangles arrived and was placed on the table along with two delicate pats of butter. 'So, what was it then? An affair? A theft?' Her eyes glinted. 'A murder?'

'It was...' Beatrice still couldn't bring herself to voice the words out loud. The memories of that night were too overpowering, too strong. She had done it deliberately, had known exactly what game she was playing. Her eyes had been wide open. Her actions had got her what she wanted, but then she had received an unexpected extra too. Something she hadn't counted on. Something that had come back to haunt her now. And if the world found out, it would threaten everything that she was trying to achieve. What she had done didn't fit with her rise to become a Dame, to become the queen of the nation's hearts.

Marg was watching her, bright-eyed. 'Is it something that you'd rather didn't make it out into the cold light of day?'

'Exactly.' Beatrice smiled gratefully, picking up a raisin Danish and taking a first bite.

'And is someone aware of it? And making things difficult?'

Beatrice nodded, sliding the name of the person she had met in the cafe across the table.

Marg read the name and nodded. Then she screwed the paper up into a tiny ball and put it into the pocket of her navy tailored trousers. 'And would you like me to... dissuade them from making your life difficult?'

'I would.' Beatrice nodded. 'Yes. If you can.'

Marg took two lumps of sugar from the tiny pot in front of them and dropped them into her coffee, using the tiny silver tongs provided. 'By any means?'

Beatrice flinched, but then steeled herself. Once upon a time there was no way she would ever have sanctioned murder, but desperate times called for desperate measures. This secret could not come to light. 'No, not quite.'

'So heavy discouragement, then? A baseball bat rather than a gun?'

'Yes. Please.' Beatrice swallowed down her mouthful of pastry with more than a little difficulty. 'This is delicious.' She thought of the shock her earlier companion would get later today and smiled to herself. They deserved everything they got.

'And are you sure that you don't want them stopped altogether?' Marg frowned. 'So that your secret, whatever it may be, never comes to light?'

'I am.'

'I see.' Marg nodded and Beatrice knew that she really did. Marg had seen enough of life – and death – to understand what Beatrice's reticence really signified. But Marg never asked any unnecessary questions – Beatrice loved her for that.

'So, can I leave it with you?'

'Consider it done.' Marg nodded. 'I just have... one favour to ask in return.'

'Oh yes?'

'That you reserve me my usual box for opening night tonight.'

'Already done, Marg.' Beatrice checked her gold watch and saw that it was nearly time for rehearsal. After yesterday's disaster, including the light crashing onto the desk, she had called the entire cast back in today for another dress rehearsal. The curtain wasn't going to go up until she, Beatrice Butler, was happy with the performance. She didn't care how long it took. She didn't care how much they moaned. She was the director and they would have to shut up and listen to her.

Marg brushed crumbs off her fingers. 'Is there anything else?'

Beatrice thought of the meeting that was coming up later. 'Well, maybe. Do you still have your council contacts?'

'Of course.' Marg poured more cream into her coffee. 'Why? Do you need some extra help to get things signed off?'

Beatrice should have known that her friend would understand. 'I do.'

'Consider it done.' Marg reached for another pastry. 'Now, off you get to rehearsal. I know that you're under pressure. And I hope you've got your light fixings sorted out. We wouldn't want any more falling down, now, would we?'

'How did you know about that?'

'I know everything.' Marg smiled. 'I thought you'd learnt that by now?'

'I can stay longer, Marg.' Beatrice drank some more coffee.

Marg shook her head. 'You've got that twitchy look – the one you only get on opening night.'

'Oh, I...'

'And I have a room booked upstairs for me and Carlo.' Marg beckoned the young man with the muscles across. 'So it's time for you to scram.'

Beatrice did so, at speed. Back on the high street of Sunshine Sands, she exhaled, her shoulders relaxing for the first time in days. With Marg on board, everything would work out the way she wanted it to. The agreement would be signed, and her secret would stay hidden. She was back in the driving seat. Tonight, the curtain would go up on her final show. It would be a triumph, just as she had planned. If the doctors were right, and her life was going to end in a matter of months, then she was going to go out on a high.

Now all she had to do was to keep the cast tensions cooking nicely – to fuel the flames so that everything would explode on stage tonight, just as she had planned.

It was going to be quite the show.

ACT TWO

THE SHOW MUST GO ON

15

CLIO

'Well, that was quite the first night, wasn't it?' Clio zipped her bright red coat up to her chin, digging her fingers into her bag of chips and dipping them onto the plate of ketchup that sat beside her on the pier. She kicked her legs out over the edge. 'Not quite the fun Christmassy night out we were hoping for, but there was definitely enough drama to be going on with.'

Next to her, Jeanie was steadily working her way through an enormous bag of scampi. The staff at the Codfather knew the three of them well, and always doubled the portion sizes whenever they came in. That had been particularly true this evening, as the owner of the best fish and chip shop in Sunshine Sands had inevitably heard about the events at the theatre, so was determined to feed the three of them up. Once they had all finally made it out of the theatre there had been no question that they would come here for fish and chips and a catch-up.

The little shop glowed behind them, still full of customers despite the lateness of the hour, chatter rising and falling as the theatrical community ate their fill after the hours of lockdown in the theatre. Clio licked her salty lips, enjoying the lilting sound of the waves far below them, lapping gently at the pier supports. Lights twinkled across the bay, for once she had a coat on that actually kept out the cold, and Jeanie's light-up Christmas pudding beanie was making her smile.

She raised her can of Coke in the air. 'To Beatrice Butler.' She heard Ross laughing behind her and wondered again about the phone conversation she had overheard. Could he be the killer? And if so, why? She checked her watch. Only half an hour to go until he was due to meet whoever he had been talking to on the phone.

Amber and Jeanie tapped their cans to hers. 'To Beatrice Butler.'

Clio carried on. 'May she rest in peace, the old cow.' She sipped, enjoying the sugary fizz on her tongue. 'Though of course she won't RIP because she'll be so unbelievably pissed off that anyone had the gall to kill her. And that she only got a one-minute slot on the BBC news, whereas Dame Maggie Smith got longer.' She smiled. 'You can bet that she's still chalking up things like that from beyond the grave. She'll be raging. It wouldn't surprise me if she haunts the BBC for ever.'

Jeanie balled up her chip paper and lobbed it into the overflowing bin next to them. 'I feel so much better after that. That was one long night. The twins are going to be unspeakable tomorrow. When I dropped them home before coming here, Tan and I agreed we'll have to do *Rock, Paper, Scissors* to decide which one of us has to look after them.'

Amber nudged her with an elbow. 'You could just say you're out on an investigation.'

Jeanie looked at her, eyebrow raised. 'I had a feeling you were going to say that.'

Amber shrugged. 'Well, we were there when it happened. It's like... fate.'

Clio felt a rush of amusement. 'Amber. This isn't a Bad Girls case – we're not going to be paid. This is a Mistletoe Murder Club case!'

Amber inhaled. 'You're not going to stop with that name, are you?'

'Nope.' Clio shook her head. 'The gun had mistletoe on it, for goodness' sake! It has to be that name.'

Amber ran a gloved hand through her hair. 'Well, seeing as you're our undercover agent, as you're in the show and everything, I suppose we can go with it.'

Clio shrugged. 'If the show goes ahead, that is. I think they'll just abandon it now Beatrice is gone.'

Amber frowned. 'That doesn't make sense. All Beatrice's directing is done. You all know where you're standing, what you're saying. And there must be an understudy for her role, surely?'

Clio smiled. 'It's Sylvia, the costume designer. And the front end of the cow, of course. I don't know if she's learnt the lines yet though. But yes, I guess we do all know our blocking – that's true.' She tipped her head back and inhaled. 'Apart from Dexter Buchanan, of course.'

'Well, I think you should do it. The show must go on, mustn't it?' Amber put her rubbish in the bin and stood up. 'Walk with me, you two. I want to compare notes.'

Clio got to her feet, tiredness making her movements heavy. It had been one hell of a day. She checked her watch, seeing that it was now 11.45 p.m. They had to be hiding at the end of the pier by midnight, so they could see who Ross was meeting. Maybe that would lead somewhere useful.

Clio grabbed her friends' hands. 'This way.'

Amber and Jeanie looked at her, puzzled.

'Come on!' They started to follow her, just as she had known they would. This is why they were her best friends – because they would follow her wherever she led, no matter what. That kind of trust was golden. That kind of trust was the bedrock of the newly formed Mistletoe Murder Club. She grinned at the two of them. They might all be knackered, pouchy and 90 per cent chips, but none of that mattered. What mattered was that they would do anything for each other. What mattered was that Jeanie and Amber were Clio's ride or dies.

They walked away from the Codfather, making their way along the pier, which was in peak Christmas mode, covered in large plastic bunches of holly, endless candy canes and – just by the Big Wheel – a huge inflatable Santa, who was in danger of losing his mooring and taking his reindeer up into the stratosphere with him. They walked past the huge slides that were full of screaming kids in the daytime, past slot machines with the claws that never actually let you pick up any of the fluffy toys on offer, past silent candyfloss stands and a shuttered coffee shop decorated in pink wooden hearts and tinsel.

Clio knew this place like the back of her hand – the scene of many teenage dates, pretending to be impressed as boys failed to win teddy bears for her, of her and Bez holding hands as the sun set while they sipped Fanta and blew Hubba Bubba bubbles at each other. She wondered whether he was all tucked up with his girlfriend Tiara now. The thought gave her a pang of something she didn't quite understand, a sinking inside her that seemed to make no sense. It wasn't like she was in a relationship with Bez, was it?

'Hey, you guys. Wait for me!' They turned to see Melissa approaching at a rapid speed, sporting a woolly hat depicting a reindeer face with antlers rising either side.

'Typically understated, I see.' Amber rolled her eyes.

'Hi, sis!' Clio smiled at the way Melissa totally ignored how much Amber hated hugging, throwing her arms around her long-lost relative. 'How's it going? Getting your Christmas on yet?'

'Hardly.' Amber extricated herself as quickly as she could.

Clio also loved the way Melissa ignored Amber's grumpiness. 'I heard what went down at the theatre. I can't believe it. I got stuck on the island, so I wasn't able to get over in time to take backstage pictures, like we agreed. But I got a few from yesterday. Maybe they might show something?'

'Great.' Amber's voice was warmer now. 'Are they on your phone? Can I look now?'

'Nah. Sorry.' Melissa shrugged. 'I was out of battery, so I popped over to yours and left it in your caravan to charge.'

Amber stopped. 'How did you get in?'

Melissa shrugged. 'I had a key made, of course.'

'Who said you could do that?'

Melissa smiled. 'We're family. I'm allowed.'

Amber had never looked less happy.

Clio decided to change the subject. The investigation. Amber would always want to talk about the investigation. 'We're heading this way because I overheard something while I was waiting to be interviewed.'

'Oh yes?'

Clio mentally congratulated herself. She had diverted a potential sisterly spat and got Amber back on to the subject of who had killed Beatrice Butler.

Amber whispered in her ear. 'I know you're trying to distract me. We'll talk about this later.'

Damn.

'This is big. Ross was in the Codfather, so I had to wait to tell you.' Clio decided to brazen it out. 'I heard Ross – at least I think it was him – talking to someone on the phone in the dressing room next to me. And it sounded like he might have killed Beatrice.'

'Ross?' Jeanie's voice was so loud that Clio checked over her shoulder to see if he was following them. Fortunately, the pier appeared deserted. 'Surely not. He seemed really lovely.'

Clio sighed. 'I know. He was saying how *he said he'd sort it*, and how *she's out of the way now*. But I can't believe it was him. Not my friend Ross. Which is why we're going to hide and see who turns up to meet him at midnight at the end of the pier.'

'This is so exciting!' Melissa punched the air. 'I'm a Bad Girl.'

Clio felt Amber stiffen beside her. 'No. You're a member of the Mistletoe Murder Club! Now, let's hide, before he gets here.'

Jeanie indicated Clio's bright red coat. 'I'm not sure you're dressed for hiding.'

'It's okay. I've got it all figured out.' Clio took her by the hand. 'We can hide inside the waltzers.'

'What?' Jeanie's voice rose in fear. 'I hate the waltzers. I always puke when I go on them. Remember what happened on my eighteenth birthday?'

'I do. And probably so does the man you puked on.' Clio sidestepped the flimsy gate that led to the fairground section of the pier. 'But the waltzers aren't going to be moving, are they? So you've got nothing to worry about.'

'OK.' Jeanie still sounded worried.

Clio squeezed her arm. The four of them wound their way past the rides, silent now, for fear they should alert whoever was waiting at the end of the pier. They walked past the Ghost Train, where Clio had thrown herself into Bez's arms at the appearance of a particularly scary ghoul, which had led to a kiss which had led to so much more, including the arrival of their beautiful Nina, who was due back in town on Christmas Eve. Clio felt herself unfurl at the idea of holding her daughter in her arms again. She was delighted that Nina was enjoying university so much, but had been gutted when a late exam had meant that her girl hadn't been able to make it home for the opening night. Maybe it was just as well, given what had happened. But she couldn't wait to see her, to hug her, to smother her in all the kisses that she had been holding inside for so long.

They reached the waltzers, which were protected by a totally ineffectual chain which had slid to the floor as if it had given up already. They climbed inside the one closest to the end of the pier, decorated in stars and rainbows, where Clio could see the lights of the Isle of Wight twinkling in the distance.

Melissa spoke in a loud whisper. 'This isn't a waltzer. This is a tilt-a-whirl!'

Amber spoke fast, pulling her down. 'Whatever you Americans call it, the point is we need to be quiet.'

'Did we all need to get in the same waltzer?' Clio's knees were cold on the metal base, her neck cricked low as she tried to duck down out of sight.

'Ow!' Jeanie winced as Clio elbowed her in the head. 'Watch out!'

On Clio's left Amber just hunkered down quietly, silent as a ninja, waiting. Beside her, Melissa's teeth gleamed as she smiled, clearly having the time of her life.

The wind moaned quietly, not sounding like it was in a Christmas mood, the air heavy, as if it was about to snow again. Footsteps went past them and the four of them stiffened and went quiet. Clio decided now was not the time to mention that Amber's elbow was pressing against her eyelid, nor that Jeanie's bum was pretty much on top of her face. She breathed in the damp fabric of Jeanie's coat and listened as the footsteps went past them and headed towards the end of the pier. Was it Ross? All Clio could see was the back end of Jeanie, so she had absolutely no idea.

Silence fell as the footsteps faded away. Amber's elbow became even more painful as her friend raised her head and peered out.

'What can you see?' Clio hissed.

'Not a lot.' Amber leant out further, craning her neck to see what was happening. 'But whoever it is, they're heading to exactly the spot you talked about, I think.'

'Who's with them?'

'No one yet.' Amber swung back in next to Clio. 'But I think I hear someone else coming now. Get down.'

'I am down.' This time Amber landed on top of Clio's leg, her chin pressing into Clio's thigh. Dear God. Clio was all for close friendship, but this was too much.

'There's a flaw in our plan.' Amber's voice was so low Clio could barely hear it.

'Only one?' Clio tried to get a nostril clear of Jeanie, but failed, sinking back again.

'Yes.' Amber shifted slightly. 'You're the only one who knows what all the cast and crew look like.'

'Oh.' Clio realised she was right. 'And I can't see anything.'

'Exactly. So we need to switch.'

'But they're right close by, yes?'

'Exactly. But we have no choice.' Amber's whisper rang with determination. 'So let's do this.'

'Are you sure?'

'I am.'

Clio took a deep breath. 'Then okay.'

Amber silently climbed out, and Clio did her best to do the same. Her back cracked loudly and she froze, but there was no reaction from the distant figure on the edge of the pier. It certainly looked like Ross. Clio's heart sank as she moved closer to him, crouching low so that she wouldn't be seen.

Clio now had a clear line of sight to the figures at the end of the pier. She could see a man who looked very like Ross. Brown hair. And something about the set of his shoulders was 100 per cent him. She wanted to call his name, to get him to prove it wasn't him. Instead, she eyed the figure approaching him, walking with big loping strides. Hood. Big coat. Wide shoulders.

The sea was louder here, so when the two figures met, Clio had to crane to hear what was being said. Arms were flying through the air, arcing, as Ross and his companion got more and more angry with each other. Clio had to get closer so she could listen in. She turned to her friends, pointing her finger to the duo, trying to indicate what she was about to do. Jeanie reached out to stop her, while Amber nodded, understanding exactly what Clio was planning and why.

She crept towards the figures, hiding behind a huge reindeer inflatable just behind them, which had the dubious job of advertising 'Bob's Christmas Burgers – your entire Christmas dinner in one bap.' She arched towards the pair, hoping that they would be too immersed in their argument to notice her.

'I did what you asked. She's gone now. She can't get in the way any more.' Clio sighed inwardly. Yes, that was definitely Ross speaking, and it sounded like he was talking about Beatrice Butler. 'So what's the problem?'

His companion was male, with a deep voice. 'She can still get in the way.'

'What? But she's dead, so...'

Clio felt a twist inside her. Ross was saying he had killed Beatrice, but still, she couldn't believe him. He hated getting a speck of dirt on one of his floral shirts – how could he cope with all that blood? With being face to face with his target? No way.

Ross's companion was speaking again. 'It turns out that Beatrice saw you coming.'

'What do you mean?'

'She had already done a deal when she died. It was all signed. All sealed. And – do you know what?'

'What?' Ross's head was down now, and Clio could only imagine what he must be feeling.

'We could have overturned it, given a bit of time and effort. But now that she has been killed – at the theatre – there is nothing we can do.'

'What?' Clio saw Ross put a hand to his forehead, saw him lean over. 'Why?'

'It doesn't matter. The fact is you haven't done your job.' The man took a step forward.

'I have.' Clio could hear the note of fear in Ross's voice. 'No one could have done more.'

'Oh, they could. Anyone would have done better than you.' The voice was getting more gravelly now, more intense. The man was closing in on Ross, and all there was behind him was a flimsy gate that should have been replaced decades ago. 'And we'll have to work out what to do with you now, won't we?'

Ross was holding up his hands, as if terrified. 'What do you mean, what to do with me?'

One more step.

'Ooh. I don't know. What do you think? What would you do with someone who has let you down?' Another step. 'Who has totally screwed up?' Ross was shifting backwards, faster now.

The man took one more step. 'Who...'

And then Ross hit the edge, the flimsy gate collapsed, and he fell backwards, screaming, into the freezing depths of the sea.

16

AMBER

'What on earth are you three doing here?'

DI Marco Santini stood, arms folded, on the pebbly Sunshine Sands beach, where Ross had just been fished alive from the freezing water. Marco did not look pleased to see Amber or her friends. Nothing new there. Up on the promenade, Ross was in an ambulance under several hypothermic blankets, his skin blue and his teeth chattering with cold and shock.

'We were having fish and chips.' Amber stuck her chin out, looking him in the eye. He didn't need to know that they – she refused to use Clio's ridiculous Mistletoe Murder Club name – were trying to find the killer too. He didn't need to know that his earlier dismissal of her had made her want to beat him again at his own game.

'Well, hello.' Melissa appeared beside Amber, holding out her hand. 'And who's this?'

Amber cringed inwardly. Please don't let her half-sister have terrible taste in men too. Clio was quite enough to be going on with. Marco was absolutely not a good bet. Divorced, with two sons who lived in Scotland, he was best described as hapless when it came to romance.

Melissa stepped towards him. 'You're looking very smart. You haven't been out on a date tonight, have you?' Somehow her American accent enabled her to get away with saying things like this. Amber looked at Melissa's bright smile, her immaculate low ponytail, the fact that she was still wearing her reindeer hat and yet somehow still looked ready to go out on the town.

'Oh no, nothing like that.' Amber couldn't quite see in the darkness, but would put money on the fact that Marco was blushing. 'I've just finished interviewing suspects at the theatre.' He lowered his voice to his favourite press conference tones. He probably thought it made him sound more intelligent.

'Oh, so you're a police officer, hey?' Melissa took a step closer, her smile widening. 'I don't suppose you've ever worked with Amber, have you? My half-sister?'

Marco paled. 'Um. Yes. Well. We did, actually.'

Amber cut in. 'He's the one who fired me.'

Marco frowned. 'Because you broke the rules, Amber.'

'You didn't have to march me out of the building with a security detail though, did you?' Amber's head was starting to ache. Too much salty food. Too many memories.

Melissa held up her hands. 'Sorry. I seem to have put my foot in it. My bad.' She laughed. 'But seeing as you fired her, Marco.' She blinked up at him. 'Might you be able to tell us anything about the case? About who your suspects are?'

Marco opened his mouth, clearly about to refuse, but Melissa spoke first. 'I mean, I'm new here, and I really want to be part of their Mistletoe Murder Club, you know?' She was twirling her ponytail around her finger, her lean body moving closer to his. 'So, can you give me any pointers?'

Marco appeared mesmerised. 'I. Um. I...'

Melissa was very close to him now. 'Like, I don't know – did the person talking to Ross get away? We lost them on the pier – just couldn't keep up, you know?'

Marco frowned. 'What person?'

'So they did, then.' Amber frowned. 'I thought they would. I wish I knew who it was.'

Marco took a step forward. 'Seriously, what person? And where?'

'They were talking to Ross over by the waltzers.' Amber shrugged, deliberately casual. 'The four of us were just hanging out, you know? Me, Clio, Jeanie and Melissa. And there was a man with Ross. Didn't he tell you?'

'He is too cold to be interviewed, so no, not yet.' Marco sounded sulky now.

Amber approached him, beckoning Clio who was standing with Jeanie further up the beach.

She grinned at Marco. 'I would tell you what they talked about, if you decided to help me by telling me... the results of the post-mortem? I know you'll have rushed it through.'

Marco puffed out his cheeks, exhaling loudly. 'And if I don't share them, will you just ask Marg Redfearn to pass them on? I know she's helped you in the past, hasn't she?'

'I might ask her.' This reminded Amber that she had not received an answer to the text she had sent Marg earlier. She kept her gaze on Marco, seeing now how tired he looked. Amber sometimes thought he had done her a favour, firing her all those months before. She preferred running her own business, preferred not being at anyone's beck and call, preferred having a choice of what cases to pursue and a free rein to choose her own approach to each one.

Right now, Marco did not look like a man who had a choice. He was the overall boss of the local detective force and yet here he was in the small hours, on the scene, in person. There had been some huge cutbacks recently, slashes in government funding and local council funding too, and now, added to his plate, was a high-profile investigation into the murder of a national treasure. It was almost enough to make Amber feel sorry for him, if only he hadn't humiliated her so acutely in the past.

She looked up, seeing flashbulbs going off from the cordoned-off press and onlookers on the pier. The media was very interested in this case, which meant Marco would be very interested in the information that Clio could give him.

She tried one more time to play nice. 'Come on, Marco. We can help you out. We overheard what they said, and it might help. And you need to solve this case and fast. Clio can be your eyes and ears on the cast.'

Clio smiled. 'That I can. Jaxon's summoned us all to The Ovation to talk about whether the show goes ahead or not. I can see who's looking suspicious, talk to Ross, try to figure out what's going on.'

Amber nodded, desperate to persuade Marco to give something away. 'She's perfect. The killer would never suspect her. She's already in the cast. So...' She stuck her hands in her pockets, wondering again where Ross's companion had gone. By the time they had called the police and the lifeguard to get help for him, the person had disappeared. Luckily, help came fast, and the searchers had found Ross clinging to the underside of the pier, tears pouring down his face, muttering through chattering teeth about how none of this was his fault. The press would have a field day with him in the morning, and Amber was sure that the internet was already starting to share memes of him hugging the pier and crying. He had every chance of going viral, not in any kind of way that he would want.

'So, Marco, how about it?' Melissa somehow made this sound like an invitation to got to dinner.

'Well. All right then.' Marco glanced around, checking that no one was listening. 'There was nothing surprising in the post-mortem, okay? She died from a gunshot wound to the head.' He spoke so quickly that Amber nearly missed his words. 'But there was something surprising in the mince pie that was at her side. Poison.'

Amber blinked. 'What? It was poisoned?'

'Yes.' He nodded. 'And so was the sherry.'

'No.' Clio gasped, her hand flying to her mouth. 'Both things were poisoned?'

Amber stared at Marco. 'What with?'

'The poison was from mistletoe berries. Crushed into the sherry and cooked into the mince pie.'

Clio was about to combust. 'Oh my God! So we *are* the Mistletoe Murder Club! I was right all along!'

Marco continued, talking fast. 'She didn't eat or drink any of it though – there was nothing in her system to indicate that. So it seems that either three different people were trying to kill her, or that one or two people were very, very determined indeed.'

'Wow.' Amber digested this. 'So who are your main suspects? Who delivered the mince pie?' She moved closer to him, so there was no danger of being overheard.

'Our main suspects? Well, it turns out everyone hated her, so it's a very long list.' He counted off on his fingers. 'But Dexter and Kylie were together in their dressing room and Gawain, the set designer guy, said he saw the two of them coming out of the dressing room together, after you and Clio managed to remove him from Beatrice's dressing room. So those two look pretty unlikely. And neither of them has a motive, that I can establish.'

Jeanie appeared at their side. 'I heard someone telling Beatrice they hated her, when I was searching for the kids backstage. It was definitely a woman. It was just before seven, I think? And Winnie – the stage manager – told me that Beatrice was deliberately stirring up trouble in the cast. Like making out that Sylvia was seeing someone else so Jaxon would dump her. That kind of thing.'

Marco looked puzzled. 'Why on earth would she do that?'

Jeanie shrugged. 'I don't know. But she was terminally ill. Did you know that?'

'You what?'

'Yeah. Cancer. Winnie told me.'

'The quiet woman with the fringe?'

'Yes.' Jeanie nodded. 'That's her.'

'She didn't tell me that when I interviewed her.' Marco frowned. 'I wonder why not.'

Because you're a crap listener, thought Amber. 'Anything else?'

'Just something about a missing ruby ring. Know anything about that?'

'No.'

He watched her for a long moment. 'You're lying.'

'No, I'm not.'

'Really?'

Amber nodded. 'Really.'

Clio gave a big yawn. 'Lots of stuff has been going missing backstage during rehearsals: wallets, jewellery, watches. Someone really needs money. Which reminds me. I found a betting slip. No name on it, but five grand on a horse called Hoof Hearted, which lost at the races today. It never made it past the first fence.'

'Wow.' Marco sucked in air through his teeth. 'So maybe whoever placed the bet stole the ring to cover the loss, and Beatrice wouldn't play ball, so they shot her.'

Amber sighed. Marco did love to jump to conclusions rather than putting in the groundwork, and here he was, doing it again.

'Boss!' An officer approached from the beach. 'Ross King has been checked over by the paramedics and is ready to be interviewed now.'

'Great. See you soon, ladies.' He stopped. 'It's lovely to have met you, Melissa.'

'Likewise.' Amber stared. Was Melissa... simpering?

The minute Marco had crunched away, Melissa tapped Amber on the arm. 'Who *is* that hottie?'

Clio looked around. 'What hottie? Where?'

'That one.' Melissa pointed at the departing Marco.

The three old friends stared at her in shock. Then Clio stepped forward and placed her palm on Melissa's forehead. 'Are you sure you didn't have any of the dodgy mistletoe sherry?'

'No. He's gorgeous. So tall and – masterful.'

'Ewwwww.' Amber couldn't deal with this. Even without being gay he was 100 per cent not her type.

Melissa stared after him, dreamily. 'Does he ride horses?'

Amber grimaced. 'What?'

'He would look amazing on a horse. So Mr Darcy.' Melissa gave a low sigh.

'Can we focus please?' Amber clapped her hands. The case. That was what she wanted to think about. Not Marco and Melissa on a date. Her one blood relative dating the man who fired her, and all while wearing a pair of antlers on her head.

She needed to take charge. 'OK, so Clio, you're on-site tomorrow with the cast, getting what information you can. I wonder about Dexter and Kylie – sure, they're going to say they were together, but is it true? I don't know. We also need to find out more about why Ross and his friend wanted Beatrice out of the way. What was she blocking? And what did she sign just before she died?'

'It must be something to do with the theatre.' Clio unsuccessfully tried to skim a stone across the gentle waves. 'Ross is an estate agent, so he could be involved in the new development, maybe?'

Amber nodded. 'And try to find out who is stealing stuff. Because this feels like an impulse kill to me – too messy, too gory. No killer wants that. So maybe someone got desperate.'

'Will do.' Clio smiled. 'The Mistletoe Murder Club is really taking off, isn't it? I might get T-shirts made. Just the initials in spangly letters. Maybe a big Christmas pudding. They'll be so festive, you'll love them, Amber.'

'NO.' Amber would not be distracted. 'Meanwhile, Jeanie and I can try to work through the rest of the clues, see what other evidence we can find, get some background on Gawain and Winnie and everyone.'

'I just don't know.' Jeanie was stalling, Amber could see it. She had done the same whenever the three of them had gone to the pub underage, pretending she couldn't find something in her bag so that she wasn't the one who had to go up and ask for the drinks. Jeanie enjoyed life inside the box, staying in the lanes, knowing what tomorrow would bring. If there was ever proof that opposites attracted, Jeanie's friendship with Amber and Clio was it.

'Let's just see where it leads, okay?'

'Maybe.' Jeanie bit her lower lip. 'But...'

Clio put a hand on her arm. 'It's because of the twins, isn't it? You feel bad about them being involved today.'

Jeanie nodded, a tear rolling down her cheek. 'I feel terrible. I'm the worst mum in the whole wide world.'

'Okay.' Amber realised she'd have to go easy. 'Well, how about we do it differently this time. You can do social media research – from home. And I'll try to get hold of some of those diaries if I can. See what you can find in those. Go through the whole cast, work out anything that might prove useful. I bet Kylie posts on socials about twelve times a day.'

'And she has a YouTube channel.' Jeanie's mouth curved up at the corner.

'Of course she does.' Amber grinned. 'And of course you've already started looking.'

'Only a little bit.' Jeanie arched her eyebrows. 'How about I come into the office in the morning and we can run through everything? I want to look into Winnie too. I think there's something odd about her working for Beatrice at all – something isn't adding up.'

'Perfect.' Amber felt a rush of excitement which just about blotted out the horror of her half-sister making eyes at her old boss. 'Now, you three. Off you go and get some sleep. You look absolutely terrible.'

'Speak for yourself, lady.' Melissa looked longingly at Marco, who was now by the ambulance. 'I'm going to—'

'Come home with me.' Amber tucked her arm firmly into Melissa's. 'That's what you're going to do.'

'Spoilsport.' They crunched over the pebbles for a moment in silence. Then Melissa piped up. 'Can we play Pin the Nose on Rudolph when we get back?'

'No.'

'How about Christmas Pictionary?'

'No.'

'Or charades?'

'No.' Amber kept moving, wishing that she had just left Melissa with Marco after all.

17

CLIO

Jaxon was trying to conduct the world's most challenging cast meeting while also eating a raisin Danish, and it was not going well.

'Look, we just need to decide...' A raisin exploded from his lips and landed in the middle of Sylvia's flat white. She gave him a look that would freeze lava and the entire meeting was in danger of grinding to a halt until she calmly picked it out and flicked it at his face. Clio and the rest of the cast held their breath, expecting an explosion, but Jaxon just brushed it away and carried on talking. Unusual. Normally, Jaxon was as flammable as Clio's daughter Nina's childhood Christmas fairy costume.

Ross was here too, turning up early, much to Clio's surprise. He was never early, and she would have assumed he'd be even less so, given his unexpected swim the night before. Clio had picked up her coffee from the bar of The Ovation and gone over to try to talk to him about what she had overheard on the pier and in the dressing rooms, but he was not in a talkative mood. His face was pale and his hair unusually dishevelled. She wondered why the police hadn't arrested him, seeing as she had heard him apparently confessing to killing Beatrice Butler. Maybe he had changed his story. There was more going on, and Clio itched to find out what it was. She had tried to ask him if he was okay after his dunking the night before, but he just shook his head and held a finger to his lips, his eyes widening in what looked very much like fear.

Jaxon held his hands wide, staring around the assembled cast and crew with dull eyes. 'So, everyone, I thought it would be useful to get together, in the wake of the tragic events of last night, to decide what we're going to do. Does the show go on, in Beatrice's honour? Or is it time to bring the curtain down on this production? Can we even do it without her? We are a small cast, hand-picked by Beatrice herself, and none of the dancers are really familiar enough with the script to step onto the stage tonight, so we would have to fill Beatrice's role from within. Sylvia, you are her understudy, so what do you think?' He couldn't look his ex-girlfriend in the eye. 'It's a tough one, isn't it?'

Clio took another sip of her coffee, which was badly needed after the antics on the pier last night. Sylvia stared at the table, her blonde hair covering her face, so Clio looked around at her fellow cast members, who were in various stages of shock. She saw that she would have to be the one who spoke first. 'Well, of course we're going to go ahead. It's what Beatrice would want, isn't it?'

Sylvia shook her head. 'No. Beatrice would hate it. Us going ahead? Without her? No way. She would think we're disrespecting her.' She folded her arms. 'I think we can safely say she would be turning in her grave if we go onstage tonight.'

'I don't know.' Kylie screwed her face up in a desperate attempt to frown through the Botox. 'This pantomime is, like, her legacy? It's the one thing she's got left to give the world? It's our chance to pay homage to her.'

'No, it's not.' Ross shook his head. 'The media circus out there is her legacy. They are going mad for this story.' He indicated the noise outside, where the country's press had settled in for the duration. On Clio's arrival at The Ovation this morning she had been hounded by journalists with huge microphones and cameras, who had spotted the actors heading towards the pub from their position outside the theatre. Now that the entire cast were holed up in here, the owner of the pub was making a killing on coffee and bacon sandwich orders from the press outside. Ross turned his coffee cup round and round on its saucer. 'Beatrice would have loved all this attention.' He sighed mournfully. 'Look, I think it's clear that we need to call this whole thing off. Beatrice is gone. It would be disrespectful to go ahead without her.'

As a man who also absolutely adored attention, this statement was out of character, to say the least. If Ross wasn't guilty of killing Beatrice, then there was definitely something else going on. Those threats last night were getting to him. Clio looked at him more closely, noticing his bitten nails, his puffy eyes. She had to get the cast to go ahead, so she could find out more. She took a deep breath.

'Actually, I think it would be disrespectful to cancel the show now she's gone. She would tell us to fight on. Beatrice Butler never turned her back on a battle – she just kept on going, guns blazing.' She realised that wasn't her finest analogy ever and rapidly moved on. 'She would have sat here and told us to get up on that stage and to give it our all, wouldn't she? She would have said that we have a full house and that we can take a collection at the end for the cancer charity she's supported since Florian died.' She looked at the lacklustre expressions around her and felt a rush of frustration. 'Come on, everyone. Where's your motivation? Where's your energy? We have to do this.'

Sylvia shook her head. 'No way. I don't know half the lines, and I'm not really an actress anyway.'

A snide voice cut in. 'Oh, I wouldn't say that.'

Sylvia glared at Jaxon. 'What does that even mean?'

Clio remembered what Jeanie had told them about Winnie stirring the pot between these two, at Beatrice's instigation. It had worked an absolute treat.

Clio jumped in. 'You'll be fine, Sylvia. I'll help you learn your lines.'

Sylvia tilted her head, considering. 'It *is* a nice costume, I suppose.'

Jaxon rolled his eyes. 'Of course that's what you would think about first.'

'Well, it's better than thinking about being stuck in a cow costume with you.' Sylvia's eyes flashed.

'Well, I didn't want to be with you either. I only did it because...' Jaxon's voice faded and his eyes tangled with Sylvia's. 'Oh, it doesn't matter.'

Clio could see that it really did matter a lot. She took a deep breath, knowing that she had to persuade them that the show must go on. If she didn't, they might never catch the killer. And, even though Beatrice Butler had been a total bitch, Clio knew that she deserved justice – for her killer to be found and locked away for ever.

She looked around the table, seeing Gawain and Winnie with their heads bowed, Dexter and Kylie inevitably holding hands, wondering how to unite them all. 'Come on, everyone. Don't just give up. Ticket sales have gone through the roof since she died.' She had no idea if this was true, but suspected it probably was. The press pack alone would have sold out the theatre – they would all want to be there to report live from Beatrice's legacy show, and to report any further drama if it happened. 'We will be playing to packed houses, bringing joy to the world. We could extend the run, even...'

Jaxon cut in. 'No, we couldn't. It's Christmas on Sunday.'

'Well...' Clio regrouped rapidly. 'We can at least bring joy to everyone who is due to come and see our amazing show this week, then. We can't deny the children their "it's behind yous" or their custard pies. And...' She turned to Kylie who was examining her nails with a small frown on her face. 'Kylie. There will be agents in the audience – they will come to honour Beatrice, to pay their respects. And they won't be able to resist you, will they? It's such a great opportunity for you, isn't it?'

Kylie's wide brown eyes lit up. 'I guess?'

Clio tried again. 'And Dexter. You've been very quiet. This would be amazing press for you – you could become our spokesman. Go out there and say that we're doing it for Beatrice – you know the kind of thing.'

Dexter's cheeks flushed. 'I don't know. I...'

'It could be the start of a comeback for you. This is the kind of story they love over in the States.' She smiled encouragingly. 'If you get onstage and blow the world's press away—' nothing wrong with a little exaggeration for a good cause '—then imagine where you could go next. The Globe? Hollywood? Amazon Prime?'

Dexter shrugged. 'But I've already got irons in the fire. I don't need...' Clio swallowed her irritation. He was clearly making this up, just as he appeared to be fabricating several elements of his life. The fancy red Porsche he had mentioned was probably fictitious, which was why no one had actually seen it. His designer clothes might well be from charity shops for all she knew. Dexter's image was carefully constructed, but was he a good enough actor to hide the fact that he had been prepared to get Beatrice out of the way? Clio didn't know.

But she did know that he wasn't listening to her, otherwise he would see what a golden opportunity this was.

'Kylie. Make him see!' Clio saw Kylie squeezing his hand and prayed that she would have more success.

'Babes.' Kylie kissed him gently on the lips and Clio felt a mild nausea rising. 'Let's do this together. It's what Beatrice would want.' She squeezed his thigh while leaning into him, giving him an excellent view of her cleavage.

'Well.' Dexter swallowed, his eyes glazing over. 'For Beatrice.'

Clio nodded in satisfaction. 'Great.'

But now Jaxon was frowning again, while Winnie and Gawain chewed silently on their bacon baps, eyes lowered. They seemed to be leaving the decision to the actors, as if their views didn't matter at all. Gawain was pale, a muscle flickering in his cheek. Winnie's hair was unwashed and she looked as if she hadn't slept.

Clio enjoyed the drama of it all, if she was honest. Because here they all were, all the suspects, all gathered around the table. It was very Agatha Christie, except that, at this point, Clio had absolutely no idea who had killed Beatrice. Who had taken the ring? Was that the person who had fired the pistol?

Jaxon opened his mouth. 'Well, I think maybe Clio's right.' Sylvia sat up straighter in her chair. 'Maybe the show must go on.' He tried some jazz hands, but it was so embarrassing that everyone looked the other way. Outside the window, cameras flashed. Jaxon continued. 'But I'm not being the cow. End of. If I'm going to be involved in a show in which someone's been murdered, then I want to have a full visual range. So I will take over as the director. I will step up. For Beatrice. For all of you.' He adjusted the pork-pie hat on his head and smiled. 'And I want you to stand beside me as we dedicate our performances to the legend that was Beatrice Butler!'

Clio arched an eyebrow as his speech was met with silence from the rest of the cast. This was not surprising as the last time Jaxon had interacted with Beatrice had been to argue with her about Daisy the Cow's dancing skills.

'I think Clio's right too.' Sylvia stood up, wiping her hands on a napkin, deliberately not looking at her ex. 'I'll be there tonight, but you will all have to get inside your own costumes because I'm Fairy Moonshine now.' She pointed at Clio. 'And you'd better have cleaned up your henchman costume by then. I know you wore it to the beach last night. It must be full of sand.'

'No, I didn't.' Clio shook her head.

Sylvia's long blonde hair got caught in her polo neck as she pulled it over her head. 'I saw you on Insta in the background, when Ross was coming out of the water. People were filming you, so don't you try and lie to me.'

'Oh.' Clio hung her head. 'Busted. I'm sorry. I'll give it a wipe down, I promise.'

'You'd better.' Sylvia frowned. 'So, who's going to go in the cow costume, then?'

There was a long silence.

Winnie spoke for the first time. 'I can't. I'm running the show backstage, all the lighting, the sound, everything. I would if I could, but there's no way.'

Gawain was also shaking his head. 'And I have to fly the scenery in and do the scene changes. Sorry.'

Jaxon frowned. 'And everyone else is on stage anyway, aren't they? So I don't know how we're going to do this. Daisy's on stage so much. And we can't really get away without her, can we? Everyone loves a pantomime cow. Could a couple of the dancers do it?'

Clio thought for a moment. Then a slow smile spread across her face. 'I think I know just the people to ask.' She stood up. 'I'll see you all tonight at the theatre.'

She made her way out of The Ovation, barging past the press, pausing just long enough to let them take her picture and to tell them which detective agency she worked for. No such thing as bad publicity, was there? She was walking across the car park when Jaxon went past her on his bike. She stuck a hand out to stop him. 'Jaxon. Can you just tell me something?'

'What?' The wind was so strong that his eyes were watering beneath his helmet.

'Well, it's just, how did Beatrice make you the cow in the first place? What did she have on you? Or what was she offering you?'

'What do you mean?'

'Come on, Jaxon. You've done enough directing to say no to playing a pantomime cow. You've done some telly. You've written scripts and sold them. You have no need to be a pantomime cow. It's a complete waste of your talents.'

Clio paused, hoping her flattery would have the effect she wanted it to. 'So how did she persuade you to do it?'

He shook his head. 'I can't talk about it. I signed an NDA.'

Clio leapt on this. 'So, she did have something on you? I knew it.'

Jaxon's eyes flicked to hers and away again. The press were coming towards them now. The closest journalist held out a recording device.

'Clio. Jaxon. Who do you think killed Beatrice?'

Clio held up a hand to ward them off. She moved away, indicating that Jaxon should do the same, then continued in a quieter voice, 'Jaxon, anything you tell me could help us to find the killer. Come on. You can trust me.'

He sighed, whirling a pedal round and round beneath his foot.

'I don't know.'

'Yes, you do.'

He shook his head. 'I... I was going to write her biography – the definitive one, the last and final. She promised me full access to all her diaries, to all her letters. That was how she talked me into the production, into doing it for free too.' He gave a bitter smile. 'And being the cow was part of the deal. Which was okay, when Sylvia and I were getting on, but...' He sighed. 'Then I found out she was seeing someone else, didn't I? So suddenly Daisy the Cow lost her appeal.'

Clio felt a pang of sympathy.

'And did you get hold of the diaries?'

'Yeah.' He nodded. 'There are some still in her dressing room – I'm guessing the police have got those, but I've got loads of the other ones in my flat, plus a lot of the letters she received from Florian when she was away on tour. But she kept me so busy I haven't really had time to get started. I was so excited about starting work, you know?'

'Any chance I could have a look?'

'Why?'

'For the Mistletoe Murder Club!' Clio gave a smile that indicated that everyone in the whole world should know what that was. 'You know?'

'Oh. Sure.' Jaxon pushed his glasses up his nose. 'I'll drop them at yours. Yeah?'

'Perfect.' That would give Jeanie something to work with. Now, Clio wanted to do him a favour in return.

'Just so you know?'

'Yeah.'

'Sylvia isn't seeing anyone else. Winnie lied. Beatrice made her.'

'What?' His bike wobbled dangerously as he took this in.

Clio nodded. 'It's true. Beatrice wanted to stir up trouble between you.'

'Oh my God.' Jaxon shook his head. 'Why? She already had me dangling, waiting for the book research interviews we were meant to do. She must just have wanted to mess with me. I know she's dead, but honestly, she was evil. She would do absolutely anything to get what she wanted.'

Clio could well believe that. She watched the way Jaxon was pulling at the button on his coat, his mouth set, his knuckles white. And she found herself wondering whether he could have been angry enough to commit murder. Whether he had looked Beatrice Butler in the eye and pulled the trigger.

Maybe Jaxon was the killer that they were looking for.

18

BEATRICE BUTLER

13.25: Six hours until her death

With Marg addressing the problem of Beatrice's blackmailer, and of the council red tape too, Beatrice was now free to focus on the production, and on the meeting that she would have after the second dress rehearsal, which was about to start.

Having got all her paperwork organised in her dressing room, she got into costume, enjoying the way the sparkly material slid over her skin, and admiring the way her body looked in the flowing dress when she examined herself in the full-length mirror in the corner of her dressing room. She saw a glass of sherry waiting on her dressing table – she always had one after lunch – and was about to pick it up when her phone bleeped.

She picked it up, peering at the screen, and saw that Marg had already come good. The councillor responsible for planning had apparently been very malleable once Marg's 'people' (aka hulks) had paid them a visit. A meeting was set up for later. Beatrice smiled to herself. First hurdle down.

She picked up her wand, reflecting on how proud Florian would be of her and of everything she was doing. She looked at the picture of the two of them together, which sat in pride of place on the windowsill, taken in that first pantomime run of 'Jack and the Beanstalk.' When he had bought her this theatre, they had promised each other that it would stand for ever, a testament to their love and to the theatrical tradition that they both adored. And so, since the developers arrived, baying for her to sign it over so they could demolish it, Beatrice had been fighting tooth and nail to keep it open. She wasn't going to give in, certainly not to that fool earlier, making that pathetic threat of exposing her past. And now, she just had one final move to make. Then she could go out there and give this show her all.

As she was about to leave her dressing room, there was a knock at the door.

'Come.'

The door opened and she saw Dexter Buchanan. She felt a rush of irritation. 'What is it?'

Dexter's pale, puffy face irritated her. In fact, his whole demeanour irritated her.

'Beatrice, I...'

Beatrice held up her hand. 'I told you. I am Dame Beatrice to you.' She needed to keep Dexter in his place. No stepping out of line. No unexpected transgressions. He was such a useful dogsbody, not to mention the other advantages to having him under her thumb. She would betray his trust in the end, of course, but he was too stupid to have worked that out yet.

He ran a hand through his ridiculous quiff. Honestly. He was in his fifties. It was time to grow up.

'Dame Beatrice, I...'

'Yes?' She folded her arms as discouragingly as she could.

'I need to ask for help.'

'I told you. No more money.'

'It's not that.' His eyes met hers. 'It's about Kylie.'

'Oh yes?' It was all she could do not to laugh. It was truly pathetic what men would do for sex. She had to admire Kylie's gumption. She had seen Dexter coming, washed-up and going to seed, and decided to rinse him for whatever she could get. Time was, Beatrice had done the same.

She pushed the memory away.

Dexter coughed. 'Your promise to give her the Beatrice Butler scholarship. At Fairview Drama School. She wants to know when you'll announce that she's the winning candidate.' He was staring at his feet now, as well he might.

'And why isn't she asking me herself?'

Dexter shifted from foot to foot.

'I think she thinks you'll say no.'

'You mean she thinks you'll have more success than her. Because you and I go way back, yes?'

'Maybe.'

Beatrice huffed impatiently. Where was his backbone? But inwardly, she smiled to herself. This was an excellent opportunity to stir up some trouble. If her plan was going to come together, she needed everyone at sixes and sevens. She had only got Dexter in for an audition because she knew how to manipulate him.

Beatrice had long made it her business to know people's secrets, and worked closely with a private investigator, initially recommended by Marg, to ensure she had a little security, once Florian was unable to watch her back any more. And it hadn't taken the PI long to find Dexter with his hand in the till, so to speak, stealing memorabilia from a director on a particularly forgettable production of 'Grease.' Beatrice had been able to intercept him, 'find' the BAFTA award, and then persuade him into doing all her dirty work.

Him falling for Kylie, or rather Kylie taking on a man well over twice her age, had been a surprise. But not necessarily a bad one. And now Beatrice was going to create havoc, setting up the huge argument that she hoped was going to make her final wish come true: her wish to make the Beatrice Butler Theatre a listed building so it could never ever be knocked down.

She smiled with a kindness that she did not feel.

'Oh, Dexter. Kylie's got this one wrong. I never promised her a thing. She's lied to you, my darling.' She shook her head, exuding sympathy. 'I'm so sorry.'

'But.' He opened and closed his mouth. 'But...'

'Silly old you. It's so easy to get caught up in these flings, isn't it? It's just as well it's only me who knows, isn't it? And don't worry. I won't tell a soul that she had you on the hook.' She gave a giggle. 'I promise!' She squeezed his shoulder. 'But honestly. The Beatrice Butler Scholarship is only for the most talented of performers. Not for amateur nobodies like Kylie. You must know that, Dexter. But it's so kind of you to fight her battles for her, isn't it? You must be careful who you trust, though, mustn't you?'

She gave a tinkling laugh, rather like Kylie's, and then held the door for him to leave. She saw the angry set of his shoulders as he headed back to his dressing room, and congratulated herself on a job well done. Several of her cast were simmering nicely, and her next step was clear. She patted the secret pocket inside her costume, in which she had placed the pistol she had brought from home.

She walked out to the wings, hovering at the props table, manned by the ever-sweating Gawain. 'Beatrice.' His voice took on that high nervous note that put her teeth on edge.

'Not now, Gawain.'

'Then when?' His face gleamed. The man really should invest in some powder. 'When can we talk?'

'Later. I have important things to do.' She swept on towards the stage. She, Beatrice Butler, had a cast to command. And she still had the rest of her life – however long that was – to make her final dream come true.

19

AMBER

Amber was in her happy place, aka standing in front of the whiteboard in her office, with a fresh coffee in her hands and a perfectly organised desk behind her. She hadn't slept much, tossing and turning feverishly in the static caravan next door, which was now her home. But a tidy-up had cleared her head. Clutter made her uneasy, and if she just kept looking at the whiteboard, she could ignore the sight of Jeanie emptying the contents of her bag onto the floor around her chair. She was trying to find one of the many mumming essentials that she always had to hand – plasters or creams or syringes full of a thick, sugary pink liquid that Jack and Yumi seemed to devour with glee. Amber took a blue pen and wrote the word 'Timeline' on one side of the whiteboard, and then 'Suspects' on the other.

'OK then.' She tapped the pen against her teeth. 'Let's do this.'

'We can start with Winnie.' Jeanie appeared to be examining her bra now. 'Oh God, there it is!' She pulled out a small silver pendant. 'Yumi must have dropped it in there when I carried her out of the childminder's. It belongs to one of the other mums, so God knows how she got hold of it. Thank goodness.' Her cheeks flushed. 'Have I told you that the twins steal things now? It's so embarrassing. The mum was really upset at drop off about losing this and I just got this bad feeling in the pit of my stomach, and...'

'Yes, you have mentioned it a few times.' Amber tried not to sound impatient. She babysat the twins once a month and genuinely had no idea how

Jeanie and Tan coped with their offspring. Amber always needed several hours in a darkened room to recover after her evenings with Jack and Yumi.

She pointed at the whiteboard. 'So. Tell me about Winnie.' She wrote the name on the right-hand side of the board.

'Winnie was trapped underneath the stage at the time of the murder, or so she told me. She said she had been locked in, but by the time I tried to get out, the door had been unbolted from the outside.' Jeanie tucked the pendant away into her wallet and zipped it shut. 'She said Gawain sent her down there, to fix the trapdoor, which he said wasn't working. Winnie found a spanner trapping the mechanism and sorted it, by which time, she was locked in.' She shrugged. 'And I have no idea if any of that's true or not as we had no trouble opening the trapdoor and jumping down into the vault beneath the stage.'

'OK.' Amber wrote this down. 'Any motive for her to kill Beatrice?'

'By all accounts Beatrice was horrible to her, but then she seems to have been horrible to everyone. She made Winnie manipulate people too, and I really don't get why Winnie said yes. I reckon Beatrice was holding something over her – it seems to have been her MO. Winnie said she worked for her because she loved being part of the industry, but I had a feeling there was more going on.'

'What kind of more?' Amber watched Jeanie closely. Her friend's instincts were rarely wrong.

'Well, just that there was more history going on than she was telling me.'

'OK.' Amber came forwards and leant back against her desk. She tried not to look at the tacky Christmas decorations that Clio had insisted on putting up all over the office. When Amber had said that this was meant to be a professional environment, Clio had just called her the Grinch and carried on anyway. But Amber hated having a bunch of mistletoe hanging over her head. She was a detective, not a Christmas card. It made her think of Clio's ridiculous Mistletoe Murder Club nonsense. She rolled her eyes and regrouped. She had to focus here.

'So why don't you start your research with Winnie? Dig around a little.'

'I already have.' Jeanie pulled out a notebook, a dog-eared orange moleskin with a pen dangling from the spine. She flicked it open. 'She doesn't do much social media, but she pops up a bit in production posts, always next to Beatrice, always eyes down, looking dutiful. She seems to be telling her who people are, some of the time? Like Emily Blunt in *The Devil Wears Prada*. And then she was in the *Sunshine Sands Post* last year, talking about life working for a theatrical legend – clearly a puff piece done for Beatrice, not her. Oh, and I did find something weird.'

'What?'

'Well, the article talks about the lovely seaside home that she inherited from her dad. But... when I checked the production files – Clio gave me access somehow – I found that she now lives in a shared house at the wrong end of town.'

'By the landfill?'

'Yes.' Jeanie nodded. 'By the landfill.'

Amber shuddered. The smell in that part of town was infamous, a choking, rotten stench that took you by the throat and never let go. 'So we need to find out why.'

'We do.' Jeanie nodded. 'And we need to talk to Gawain to find out his take on this. Did he really send her down there? Was the trapdoor really jammed? Was it all part of some plan? Maybe he's the one who made the light fall on Beatrice's desk? He's the one with the Welsh accent, right?'

'Right.'

'So he's the one I heard in Beatrice's dressing room, just before she was killed. And the one you found crying afterwards. And I heard them arguing – she was saying he was a liar. So he has to be a main suspect, doesn't he?'

'He does. He may have had motive and opportunity to kill her. And the means, depending on where the pistol was kept. I'll see if I can talk to him.' Amber uncapped the pen again. 'OK, so that sounds like an interesting set of questions for Winnie and Gawain. And then we have Jaxon, Sylvia, Dexter, Kylie and Ross.'

Jeanie nodded. 'Well, it sounds like Clio is going to get information out of Ross, doesn't it?'

'Yes.' Amber nodded. 'It's weird the way no one heard the shot, isn't it?'

'Not really, given how remote the dressing room was.' Jeanie sighed. 'And then there were the words on the mirror in lipstick. And the fact that she was dying anyway.'

Amber nodded. 'I confirmed that with her GP this morning.'

'You didn't pretend to be police again, did you?'

Amber pulled a face. 'Maybe.'

'Amber. You promised you wouldn't do that any more!'

'I know. But it was in a good cause, okay?'

Jeanie frowned. 'You'll get in trouble.'

Amber shrugged. 'Not if no one finds out.' Her mind was whirring. There were too many questions and not enough answers yet. 'We just need to find one piece of the puzzle, and everything else will fall into place. Like, was there just one killer, or several would-be killers? Where was the pistol being kept? Were Kylie and Dexter really together or did one of them fake an alibi for the other? What did Beatrice sign before the show?' She put the cap on the pen and turned back to her friend.

'There are too many people moving around, and none of them were caught on any kind of camera.' Jeanie tipped her head back towards the ceiling, exhaling in frustration.

Amber drummed her fingers against her thighs. They needed to establish a timeline, some basic facts, and then connect the dots however they could until they knew who had done it. She was well aware that the police would be throwing all their resources at this too, but she knew that the three of them could do it better. She wanted to be the one to solve this.

'And then there's the other question, which is where's the ruby ring?' Jeanie leant forwards, her elbows on her knees.

'Exactly.' Amber eyed the board, working it through in her head. A missing ring. A victim who was hated by everyone, and who had been killed while a large audience was in the theatre. A thief. Several attempts at murder: the stage light, the poisoned sherry and the poisoned mince pie. Ross and his mysterious accomplice. There was no way all these things were coincidental. But they had no way in to solving the case – no guiding clue to enable her to start unpeeling the layers until they got to the truth.

She exhaled in frustration. 'OK, I'm going to go and see Winnie and then Gawain. You keep the research going – dig deeper into Kylie's socials, because she must have left some kind of clue on there. Dexter too – see if there are any other connections between him and the rest of the cast. Oh, and Clio's got some diaries and letters for you to go through – Beatrice's memoirs from her golden days. Jaxon has shared them with her – he was meant to be writing Beatrice's biography – so there might be something useful in there.'

'Great.' Jeanie was digging around in her bag again. She pulled something out, and her brow furrowed. 'Hang on.' She exhaled slowly. 'Oh God. What have they done now?'

'What?'

Jeanie held up a small gold photo frame. 'This isn't mine.'

'It's not?'

'No.' Jeanie shook her head, her curls flying. 'I did think my bag was a bit heavy. I think the twins must have stolen it. They were on the loose backstage at the theatre, and they must have picked this up somewhere.' She put the heel of her hand to her forehead. 'Oh God. I'm going to get arrested at this rate. I'm going to be locked up because my toddlers are hardened criminals and steal everything all of the time. I'll be hounded out of Sunshine Sands and they'll be in Young Offenders' Institutions by the age of ten.'

'Calm down, Jeanie. They're kids. That's all.' Amber shook her head. 'Take a breath.'

Jeanie inhaled obediently. 'Now, show it to me.' Amber held out a hand and Jeanie put the photo into it. She turned it over, examining it. 'Wow.'

'What?'

'Well...' Amber examined it. 'It's a wedding photo.' She frowned. 'And guess who's in it?'

'Who?'

'Beatrice Butler.'

'So it's *her* wedding photo?'

'No. It's not hers. I don't know who the bride and groom are, but guess who is there too?'

Jeanie watched her, eyes wide.

Amber felt a flare of excitement. 'Winnie.'

Jeanie grimaced. 'So what? She's Beatrice's assistant. She might well be there.'

'No.' Amber shook her head. 'Not Winnie now. Winnie about fifteen years ago. The teenage version. Same fringe, though.'

'Let me have a look.' Jeanie came and stood beside her. 'Oh my God, it *is* her. It looks like a family photo or something.'

'Told you.' Amber put the photo down. 'So now we have a new question.'

Jeanie's voice bubbled out. 'Are Winnie and Beatrice related?'

'And if they are, why hasn't Winnie mentioned it? And does it link to her house? The one she inherited?'

'Yes!' Jeanie's face was flushed with discovery.

'I'll get going.' Amber grabbed her coat from the hook by the door.

'And I'll get researching!' Jeanie stood up, presumably to head to Clio's caravan to find the diaries.

They both looked up as Clio burst through the door and bounded up to them.

'Clio! I thought you were meeting the cast today?'

'I was!' Clio clapped her hands together. 'And I have great news! A real chance to catch the killer!'

'What do you mean?'

'Well, not only did I persuade everyone that the show must go on, but we're going to perform the entire run – so lots of opportunity to see the cast in action, to work out who's done what, to see how they interact.'

'Yes?' Amber folded her arms. She had seen this look on her friend's face many, many times before, and generally it led to booze and Amber waking up feeling like she'd been kicked in the face by an overweight pony. No one was a more loyal friend than Clio, but no one had chaos as deeply ingrained in their soul either. Amber looked down at her clear desk and beautifully organised whiteboard. Opposites attracted, it seemed.

'So what's going on, Clio?'

Her friend looked like she might explode. 'It's brilliant, if I do say so myself. You see, we were talking about how the show must go on, but there was a problem—'

Amber and Jeanie shared a nervous glance and waited. Clio always liked to maximise suspense. Once she had awarded herself a drumroll when announcing which pizza she had bought from Sainsbury's and had been disappointed when Amber and Jeanie didn't join in.

'Because we have a gap in the cast.'

'You do?' Amber didn't see what it had to do with her.

Clio continued, her smile widening. 'Two people have dropped out of the cast – well, one is going on instead of Beatrice, to be honest.'

'Who?' Amber wondered if this might perhaps shed some light on the case.

'Jaxon and Sylvia are no longer playing Daisy the Pantomime Cow.'

'Really?' Amber felt a creeping sense of dread. Suddenly, she saw where this was going. Suddenly, she saw what Clio was talking about.

Clio nodded. 'Yes. Jaxon needs to direct, and Sylvia is Fairy Moonshine now – she did some acting years ago, so it should be okay. Which leaves a gap, doesn't it?' She smiled at them with glee. 'So I have an idea.'

Amber had a very bad feeling. 'What's this great idea, then?'

Clio was practically jumping up and down now. 'It's one of my best ever ideas.'

This didn't make Amber feel any better.

'What?'

'You two are about to make your stage debuts!'

'No. No way. Absolutely not.' Amber had always been backstage for school productions, with her and her teachers having decided mutually that to have her onstage was too much of a risk. She had even screwed up playing a tree in a nativity play aged six, when she had broken her costume coming through the door and so had simply been a small girl dressed in brown. Afterwards, one of her foster sisters had asked her why she had played a poo.

Jeanie was already shaking her head. 'No, Clio. I can't go onstage. No way.'

'Me neither.' Amber didn't have time for this. 'No. We can't do that. It's impossible. There are dances to learn, aren't there?'

'She's a cow! Of course she can't dance! You'll be brilliant!' Clio's eyes were alight with the brilliance of her own idea. She was wearing the same expression she got when she met a man who was clearly going to treat her like dirt. A man she was going to change. Amber felt dread start to trickle in her stomach.

It was time to be decisive.

'Clio. The answer is no. I will not go onstage. Drop this idea now.'

'But you'd be the cow! It's the perfect disguise!'

'No,' said Amber and Jeanie in unison. 'We are never going onstage. Not. Going. To. Happen.'

And they looked at each other, secure in the knowledge that they could say no to Clio, that she would never ever persuade them into doing this.

No. Never. No way.

Not happening.

20

AMBER

With only hours to go until her stage debut as a pantomime cow, Amber drove up to a grimy house in the less scenic part of town. She stopped the engine and sat for a few minutes, answering client correspondence, explaining to one woman that her husband did not appear to be cheating on her, while updating a male client that his daughter was most definitely stealing his valuables at a rate of at least five a week.

As she typed, Amber thought about her own family. Jeanie and Clio were like sisters to her and the three of them shared trust, loyalty and a variety of injokes – her best friends were the foundations of Amber's world, so much so that Amber had ended up saying yes to Clio and agreeing to go on stage later. And then there was Melissa, so obsessed with Christmas that her WhatsApp picture was her face superimposed onto a red holly background. Amber was still working out what to make of her, learning how to fit real family into her life. Her guard had been up for so long – it would take her some time to let it down again.

Amber pressed send on her final email and leant back in the car seat, inhaling the fresh scent coming from the cardboard lemon dangling from her rearview mirror, and looking around the vehicle that had effectively become her second home when she had started the agency. Amber almost spent more time in here than in her static caravan nowadays, her evenings and nights eaten up with shifts on surveillance, waiting for people to give themselves away, to reveal their secrets.

Refocusing, she gazed at the house where Winnie lived, seeing the rubbish bags spilling over the top of the battered black wheelie bin, the bottles piled up on the front step, the weeds choking the life out of the garden and the unkempt lawn. It looked like a classic student house, an unloved space that its occupants were passing through until degrees were gained and adult life began in a new city with a new set of keys. As Amber watched, she spotted a large rat cleaning its paws in a wilting flowerbed beneath the front window, before it dived into the pile of rubbish bags and disappeared.

It seemed an odd home to choose for a thirty-something woman. Even if Winnie had been forced to sell the house she had inherited from her parents, maybe due to debt or death duties or something else, living here still didn't quite fit. Amber got out of the car and approached the house, appreciating the cold air on her face, despite the overwhelming smell of rotting rubbish from the landfill nearby. Now she was closer, Amber could see Christmas decorations inside the house – furls of tinsel, fairy lights on a small tree, paper chains dangling from the ceiling. Clouds of steam came from an open window and Amber could smell some kind of burning. And she could hear voices too. Instinctively, Amber halted, listening. It never hurt to pick up extra information, so she decided to see what the occupants of the house were saying before making her presence felt.

'Sad?' A loud laugh followed this word. 'No. I'm not sad. She was vile.'

Amber stiffened, crouching beneath the window.

'I mean, I only worked for her because I knew that if I could survive that I could survive anything.' This was met with some muted laughter from the unseen listeners. 'I never ever liked her, you know?'

'So why does everyone love Beatrice so much, Winnie?'

A cynical laugh. 'Because she was a great actress! Total fake. End of.'

Amber blinked in surprise. Of all the things she had heard about Winnie, there had been a consistent theme. She was shy. She was quiet. She was downtrodden. Beatrice Butler owned her. So hearing this version of her was a shock. Had she just been playing a part the whole time to cover up her real intentions? Her plan to kill Beatrice?

It was time to find out. Amber rang the doorbell.

Footsteps approached and the black front door swung open. The Christmas wreath that hung on it swung out and nearly hit Amber in the face. Someone was staring out at her. Dark hair divided into pigtails, bright red lipstick, dark eyeliner, a tight pink top and combat trousers descending into stacked white Nike trainers.

'Winnie?' Amber couldn't quite believe she'd come to the right house. Mousey? No way.

'Who's asking?' Winnie's eyes narrowed with suspicion. Her voice was low. Confident. Not remotely what Jeanie had described.

'Um.' Amber was taken aback, struggling for words. 'I'm Amber Nagra. I'm a friend of Clio's.'

Winnie put her hand on the front door. 'I'm busy, so...' She made as if to swing it shut.

'I just have a few questions for you.'

'The police have already interviewed me.' Her tone was abrasive, and again Amber was surprised by how different this version of Winnie was to the ones she had heard about before. She was clearly a bit of a chameleon. 'So why should I talk to you?'

'Well.' Amber had to stop the door being slammed in her face. Clio's mad idea would have to do. 'I'm from the Mistletoe Murder Club.'

'The what?' Winnie put her head on one side, clearly intrigued.

'Um.' Amber thought hard. 'It's a local true crime group. And we're interested in what happened to Beatrice.'

'In what way?'

'Well. We've heard that there was more than one person who wanted to kill her.'

Winnie tried to push the door shut, but Amber's foot was in the way.

'And...'

Winnie frowned. Amber thanked God for Jeanie's kids' kleptomaniac tendencies. 'Because I happen to know that you were related to Beatrice.'

'What are you talking about?' Winnie gave a casual flick of her hair, but her eyes were nervous.

Amber reached into her bag and took out the photo that Jeanie had found. 'This is yours, I believe?'

Now Winnie paled. She looked to right and left, her cheeks starting to redden. 'No. That's not mine.'

'Then it's Beatrice's, isn't it?'

Winnie shuffled from foot to foot but said nothing.

'I'll take that as a yes.' Amber smiled sweetly. 'Now, can I come in? And just so you know, if you refuse, I'm going to tell everyone anyway, minus whatever reason you give me for not telling the police about your family ties to Beatrice.'

'Well, it's not as if she ever told anyone, is it?' Winnie drummed her fingers against the doorframe.

'You should still have disclosed it when you were interviewed, shouldn't you? Some people might think it's suspicious that you didn't.'

Winnie's mouth was a hard line. 'Well. Okay, then. Come in if you have to. But I didn't do anything, so you're wasting your time.'

'That's fine by me.' Amber entered the hall as Winnie stood back to give her room. The house was as depressing as she had expected, with scuffed brown carpets that showed no signs of having ever being cleaned, mouldering wallpaper, stairs with several parts of the banister missing, maybe through misuse or maybe through drunken partying – it was impossible to tell. Winnie led Amber away from where she had been talking to her friends in the kitchen, up the creaking stairs to a tiny bedroom at the back of the house. It had a dirty sash window, a bookcase full of plays and poetry, a single bed and a wardrobe. On the wall was a poster of Andrew Scott in *Hamlet*.

Winnie sat down on the bed and folded her arms belligerently.

'I don't see why it matters whether I'm related to Beatrice Butler or not.'

Amber frowned. 'I'm not sure the police would see it that way. They would see omitting that information as potentially suspicious.'

'What, and the Mistletoe Murder Club does too, does it?'

'Yes.' Amber nodded, thinking how pleased Clio would be by this reference.

'I just...' Winnie started pleating the bedcover in her fingers. 'I just didn't want people knowing. She was my great aunt, okay? My mum's aunt. They'd think I was only working for her because I was related to her. But the truth was... I was working for her because I wanted to build my contacts. I put up with all her shit, all her rudeness, all her dictating, because I wanted to get a career out of it. I played a part. And then she...' She visibly stopped herself.

'Then she what?'

Winnie sighed. 'She took my house.'

'Thought so!'

Winnie's face jerked upwards. 'I beg your pardon?'

Amber managed to restrain her huge grin. 'There was an article in the

Sunshine Sands Post about you, and it mentioned the nice house you'd inherited. Which you're definitely not living in now. So why don't you tell me what happened, Winnie?'

Winnie shrugged. 'OK.' She slumped back against the rose-patterned wallpaper. 'So, when my parents died, I inherited their beachside house. They had a lot of debt, so there was money to pay on the mortgage, and I couldn't afford it as I was still studying at uni. I was so excited to be a stage manager, you know? Couldn't wait to get out there and make the stage my career, like my Great Aunt Beatrice.' She gave a bitter laugh.

'Next thing I know, Great Aunt Beatrice turned up and hustled me out so fast my feet didn't hit the floor. She told me she'd give me a head start in the industry, she told me that she needed the house as security, like a deposit, for all the help she was going to give me.'

'But she was your great aunt?'

'She was.'

'So she could have just given it to you anyway.'

'Well, she said it would help me to be hungry, to make my way in the industry.' Winnie's mouth twisted bitterly. 'She said she was doing me a favour, taking the house, that it would lead me to do great things, that I would claw my way to the top. She said she honestly thought she was making things better for me, the lying cow.

'I later worked out she had money troubles, and taking the house and renting it out meant that she could cover the gap, for a bit. But yeah, I got angry, when I realised that she had made me sign a document that basically gave the house to her. I trusted her, you know? My parents had just died, and I was vulnerable. I didn't know that she could be so manipulative – not back then, anyway. I wish I'd worked it out earlier.'

Amber nodded, feeling a rush of sympathy.

'So yeah.' Winnie was pleating the duvet again. 'I was stupid, I guess. I shouldn't have trusted her.'

Amber watched Winnie's face. 'So what did you do?'

'Well, I didn't kill her, if that's what you mean.' Winnie's chin jutted forwards and her eyes glinted. There was a chill to her face that Amber had seen before, across the table in police interview rooms, when she had just proved that someone was guilty. 'I would never do anything like that.'

Amber held up her hands. 'I wasn't saying that you would.'

Winnie continued, her eyes not meeting Amber's. 'Even before the cancer, she was awful. She was horrible. Always has been. All those years when she was appearing on breakfast TV announcing her new charity foundation, she was smearing her fellow actresses, deliberately hiding props when they went on stage so they'd screw up, writing hate mail, sending her rivals spooky flowers to freak them out – the works.' Winnie snorted decisively. 'She was a vindictive bitch. I'm so bloody glad she's dead, though she's probably left the house to someone else, just to make sure that I never get my hands on it. You know, I never understood why she hated me, why she felt the need to keep me down for so long, but now I think that's just how she was – she wanted everyone else to hate themselves so she could shine a little brighter.'

Amber swallowed. 'Why did you never tell anyone, Winnie? Why did you carry on doing whatever she wanted you to do?'

'I had no other options.' Winnie shrugged. 'She had me trapped. She used to tell me that no one else would employ me after reading the reference she would write for me. She had me totally under her control, if I wanted to work in theatre. And...' Now her brown eyes were shining. 'That is all I have ever wanted. That feeling when you're backstage and the show is about to start. The hush from the audience. The buzz of the actors getting ready backstage. The expectation as the stage is set behind the curtain. The teamwork. It's an amazing buzz. The best. And then the applause when it all goes well, hundreds of people on their feet, clapping, all because of the magic in that room. The ovations. Knowing that the work I do behind the scenes is what brings it all together. That the actors couldn't do it without me. I bloody love it. And now she's gone I can get out there and make my name.'

The smile on her face, manic and determined, made something click into place for Amber. She thought about the poisoned mince pie and the untouched glass of sherry. About the unlocked door through to the cellar beneath the stage and the supposedly jammed trapdoor.

Winnie seemed to sense Amber's thinking. She stiffened, her eyes narrowing, like a cat about to spring.

Beneath them, there was a loud bang on the front door and a yell of 'POLICE.'

Winnie jumped up, her eyes wild. She narrowed her eyes at Amber. 'You've set me up.'

'No, I haven't!' Amber blocked the door. She wouldn't let Winnie escape.

She could have been the one to shoot Beatrice. She could have been the one to set up all three – or all four – murder attempts, if you included the falling light.

'You told them. About me being related to Beatrice. They're here for me, aren't they? Oh God.' Winnie ran to the window and started tugging it open.

'I didn't tell them anything!' Amber felt a jolt of disappointment. Marco and team had worked this one out all by themselves.

'I've got to get out of here!' Winnie finally got the sash to lift up high enough for her to stick her head out, but not the rest of her body. She tugged harder. 'Shit. It's stuck!'

Amber stepped forward 'Don't run, Winnie. It just makes you look guilty.'

'They already think I'm guilty.' The banging at the door increased in volume. 'Even though I was locked underneath the stage at the time of the murder. I have an alibi, for God's sake!'

'So you say. But Jeanie managed to get out, didn't she?'

'See? Even you think I did it!' Winnie won her battle with the window and jerked it upwards. She moved the greasy curtain out of the way and put one leg on the sill. 'I'm telling you, I didn't kill Beatrice!'

'But...'

'POLICE. LET US IN.' There was more banging. There was no way the ancient front door was going to survive much longer.

Winnie stood on the windowsill. 'I'm not staying for this.'

Amber knew there would be police down below, in the side return, hiding. Winnie would never get away. 'Don't do this, Winnie.'

But Winnie had given the window one final tug and had already jumped, landing with a smack on the paving stones below. Amber looked out, watching as Winnie tried to run, before the officers below grabbed her by the shoulders. Amber could see her flailing and fighting, then heard her scream as she was wrestled to the ground. Damn. She had so wanted to solve this one before Marco. Sighing, she walked to the front door and opened it. And there he was. DI Marco Santini, puffed up to the nines by his morning's work.

'You again?' He frowned, brown eyes narrowing. 'Funny how you always seem to be in the wrong place, isn't it?'

'Or the right place.' She looked him in the eye. 'I take it Winnie killed Beatrice, then?'

'She tried to.'

'What do you mean, tried?'

'Well, I shouldn't really tell you, but...' He clearly couldn't wait to crow about his achievements. 'We found her prints were on the sherry glass. The one that was poisoned.'

'The one that Beatrice didn't touch?'

'Exactly.'

'But that's hardly proof, is it? It's circumstantial.'

'Yes, but we also found crushed mistletoe berries hidden inside a matchbox in a drawer of the stage manager's desk just now.'

Amber made sure that her face didn't give away her surprise.

Marco continued, swelling slightly as he enjoyed his sense of having one over on Amber. 'And because Beatrice was her great aunt, who stole her childhood home from her – we have a motive. Right there.' He put his hands on his hips. 'So. I hate to say it, but... we beat you.'

'No you didn't. You still don't know who actually killed Beatrice, do you?'

'Well, it's a pretty short leap, isn't it? Winnie obviously got frustrated when the sherry wasn't drunk, so she shot Beatrice instead. The mince pie was obviously her doing too.'

'Why "obviously"?' Amber felt a surge of indignation. 'There's nothing obvious about it at all!'

'Now, Amber.' He waggled his forefinger at her, and Amber wondered yet again how she had refrained from killing him back when they worked together. 'Don't be bitter. The best man won. Accept it.'

He pulled a comb out of his pocket and started to sweep his curls back from his forehead. Then he pulled out a small compact and took the shine off his nose. Amber watched him, bemused until she heard the press vans pulling up outside, heard doors slamming, heard loud voices outside the house. Marco turned, a smile on his face.

Amber rolled her eyes. 'Marco, you didn't...'

'Didn't what?' He glanced at her.

'You didn't tip them off, did you?' Amber glanced at Winnie, still fighting as she was shoved into a police car. This wasn't fair. Winnie was being used to make the police look good, to make DI Santini look good.

His face was stern now. 'I do wish you'd stop intruding on our investigation, Amber. I have been very patient indeed in the face of your near-constant presence in this murder case, but now I have had enough. I could have you for obstruction, you know.'

Amber laughed. 'I'm not obstructing anything. All I'm trying to do is to find the killer.'

'We've already got her.' Marco flicked some lint off his shoulder. 'Now, excuse me, but I've got press to talk to.'

Amber watched, fuming, as he walked out to a sea of microphones and cameras, his face glowing with pride as he shared the news about the arrest. Amber knew there was more to this – that Marco had just taken the easy option, as he always did. She would have to show him, again. She would have to teach him how to really catch a criminal, how to dig down beyond the obvious into the hard evidence below.

Amber didn't know if Marco was wrong, but she did know that she wanted to explore the mystery further. She would talk to Gawain next and work out whether Winnie had genuinely been locked beneath the stage or not. And she would ask Marg Redfearn to share the forensic reports with her – Marg always had a hotline to whatever was happening with the police. Because if Winnie's prints weren't on the pistol that had killed Beatrice Butler, then it was possible that Amber and her friends could still find the murderer, and in doing so, they could beat Marco to solving the case yet again.

21

CLIO

Clio knew enough about Dexter Buchanan to understand that he would be wherever the cameras were. As such, when she left the betting shop she headed for the theatre, and knew, when she saw the press returning from Winnie's arrest, that he would arrive very shortly indeed. She wanted to talk to him – to ask him about the huge bet he had placed on Hoof Hearted, and to find out what he had done when his horse had fallen at the first fence, losing him five thousand pounds.

She loitered in the theatre lobby, the BestPantoEver WhatsApp chat already exploding with the news about Winnie. Amidst the exclamation marks (Ross), and the WTF face emojis (Kylie), absolutely no one but Clio appeared to have realised that they now had no stage manager tonight. They would be very lucky if the curtain went up at all. Maybe Gawain could cover it? Or Jaxon, at a push?

Clio watched for Dexter, ready to accost him as soon as he appeared. At last, a prolonged period of clicking cameras and yelled questions outside were followed by Dexter entering the theatre, his hair gleaming with wax. A waft of aftershave hit Clio so hard that her eyes started to water as she walked towards him.

'Dexter. How are you?' He stopped, clearly startled to see her.

'Fine.' He sighed. 'I just can't believe that Winnie has been arrested for killing Beatrice though.' She saw a glimmer of something like pleasure in his eyes, and wondered why. 'It's a terrible business. But...' He rallied. 'It's always the quiet ones, isn't it?'

'I guess so.' Clio nodded. 'But still, I wouldn't have had her pegged as a killer, would you? Maybe she was the best actor of us all.'

He shrugged, sipping from his portable coffee mug. 'Maybe she was. The press are going nuts out there. Such a hassle, isn't it?' She saw the small smile at the corner of his mouth and knew that he was absolutely loving the attention. It was almost as if Beatrice dying had done his career a favour. Increased attention, lots of press. That could be enough of a motive for a man whose career had taken a nosedive.

She watched him carefully. 'You can handle it though, Dexter. Can't you?'

'Of course.' He looked over her shoulder. 'You know me. Fearless. Aren't I, babes?'

Clio looked behind her to see Kylie had appeared from the door that led through to the dressing rooms, her long dark curls trailing down her back, clad only in a thin silk kimono. Her face froze when she saw him. She walked past, ignoring him. 'Hi, Clio.'

Dexter sagged and Clio saw in that moment that he really was infatuated with Kylie. Everything about him screamed it, from his big, sad eyes, to the way he instantly turned to his girlfriend, his arms wide, ready to make amends. 'You're not still angry with me, are you, babes?'

Kylie drummed long silver nails against her thighs. Clio thought she also deliberately loosened the kimono belt, so that her cleavage became even more obvious. 'I'm not angry.'

'Oh, good.' Dexter was a puppy waiting for a stick to be thrown. 'Then, are we going out tonight then, after the show? I'll take you somewhere nice.'

'No.' Kylie folded her arms. 'I'm washing my hair.'

Clio realised that she could use this tiff to find out what she wanted. She just needed to get Dexter out of the way first.

She gasped, as though suddenly remembering something urgent. 'Dexter, there were some autograph hunters in here earlier. There's a ton of stuff for you to sign on the stage.' She had dumped a load of pantomime flyers there earlier. Signing those should take him an hour or two, at least. 'They're going to auction them for Beatrice's charitable foundation. I think Claudia Winkleman is going to be the host – it'll be a proper gala evening. It's such a lovely idea, isn't it? A great thing to be associated with. Amazing for your brand.'

'Oh yes?' Dexter's face lit up, his ego not even beginning to question whether this scenario was likely or not. 'Well, I'd better get back there then. We don't want to keep the public waiting now, do we?'

'Nope.' Clio gave him a sunny smile. 'Why don't you leave me here with Kylie, and go and start signing?'

He hovered, clearly uncertain about leaving Kylie with the argument still hanging in the air. She had to get him out of the way. Another lie was required. 'I heard a couple of TikTokers are looking for you too. Millions of followers, apparently. They want to film with you, they said, to talk to you about Beatrice, your memories of her, that kind of thing? They're somewhere back there, anyway.' That would keep him looking for a while. Long enough for Clio to get what she needed.

Dexter grinned at Kylie. 'See you later, babes.'

'Whatever.' Kylie turned away. Dexter disappeared backstage, head hanging.

'So, what was all that bullshit about?' Kylie put her hands on her hips. 'There aren't any TikTokers backstage. No one wants him to sign anything.'

Clio was taken aback at Kylie's sharpness, but hid it with a smile.

'I wanted to have a little chat with you.'

'About my skincare tips?' Kylie's face lit up. 'You know, I could really help you, Clio. I think my advice could do wonders for your crow's feet, let alone the commas above your eyebrows. They're so deep.' Her eyes widened with concern. 'I mean, like chiselled in?'

Great. Clio pressed her lips together to avoid spitting out the multiple four-letter words that sprang to mind.

'Thanks for the ego boost, Kylie.' Clio made a mental note to buy better moisturiser. And to remember to apply it.

'You're welcome.' Kylie beamed. 'I'm always honest. I need to keep it real for my followers.'

'Of course you do.' Clio gritted her teeth. 'Now, listen, Kylie. I'd love to hear your skincare tips, of course. But I have a couple of questions first.'

'Oh yeah?'

'Yeah. That's why I wanted to get you on your own.' Clio finally landed on a way of getting the information she wanted, praying it would work.

'Did Dexter promise you a big present today?'

'Yeah.' Kylie's face lit up. 'He said he was going to get me this diamond bracelet I saw online, yeah? How did you know?'

Bingo.

'He just seems really into you.'

'Oh, yeah, he is.' Kylie indicated her lean body. 'I mean, it's not surprising, is it?'

'True.' Clio inhaled deeply. 'So. Can I see the bracelet?'

'Oh, no.' Kylie's face clouded. 'He never got it. He said it had sold out, but I saw it, still in the shop, when I went out for a coffee this morning. Maybe he's going to surprise me with it?'

'Maybe.' Clio didn't think so. 'So he said he was going to get it, but then didn't follow through?'

'Exactly!' Kylie nodded. 'He was sure he was going to get paid for something yesterday, he was telling me all about how we were going to go out for dinner, have champagne, all that... But then he went outside for a work call or something, and he was gone a while, and when he came back he was all grumpy and sad. He left rehearsals to get the bracelet, and came back saying it wasn't there any more.' She flicked a curl out of her face. 'I mean, what the hell?'

Clio nodded, her mind racing. It sounded very like Dexter had gone out to listen to the race, heard Hoof Hearted's fate, and then realised he couldn't get the bracelet after all. When Clio had been to the betting shop just now, the man behind the counter had been reticent, to say the least. He had refused to confirm who had placed the huge bet or to show Clio the CCTV of the transaction. However, he had let slip that the buyer had been a man by referring to the customer as 'he', so at least that had narrowed down the list to Jaxon, Ross, Dexter or Gawain.

She looked at Kylie sympathetically, aiming for one more bit of information.

Kylie was still talking. 'He always promises me things and doesn't get them. He was talking to Beatrice about the scholarship too, but I haven't heard anything. And now she's dead, I...'

Clio looked at her, uncomprehending. 'What scholarship?'

'For drama school? The Beatrice Butler Scholarship. It pays all the fees for the whole three years. Dexter said he'd sort it with Beatrice, without me having to audition or anything.' Kylie sniffed dismissively. 'But I've heard nothing on that, either.'

Thank God for that, Clio thought. Her time as an actress had been full of unfair leg-ups like this, all of them happening to other people. She kept her feelings to herself, trying a new tack.

'Did you see Dexter with a small bit of paper?'

Kylie's eyes narrowed. 'Yes. A couple of days ago. He dropped it once and freaked out. Why? I thought it was weird actually, as he doesn't normally keep receipts.'

Clio felt a wave of satisfaction. If Dexter had placed the bet, then he had lost the bet. Five thousand pounds gone. Just like that. He must be desperate to get the money back.

Kylie started talking again, as if unleashed. 'The only times he really gives me stuff is when he's nicked something.' She side-eyed Clio, as if trying to shock her. 'I mean, the day he got hold of that wallet at that black-tie event in London, we had an amazing night out.' She gave a tinkling laugh that made Clio want to put her hands over her ears. 'Oops. I wasn't meant to talk about that.' She gave her hand a little slap. 'Bad Kylie.'

Clio could see that the mention had been entirely deliberate. Kylie was angry with Dexter and out for revenge.

Kylie continued. 'I mean, he only does it because he has to.' Kylie wound a strand of hair around her fingers. 'Like, he says he has a duty, you know? To keep his fans happy?'

Wow. Dexter was clearly the king of rationalisation.

Kylie continued. 'But I'm not sure if I believe him.'

'I get it. He sounds like he's let you down.' Clio gave a sympathetic smile, while reflecting on everything she had heard. Kylie was clearly not a woman to cross. She didn't hold back in getting her revenge. As her companion wandered back across the foyer, twirling the belt of her silk kimono, Clio wondered how far Kylie would go to get that scholarship and just how focused she was on fame. Was she ambitious enough to hold a gun to Beatrice's head, to persuade her to sign the scholarship forms?

Kylie hovered at the door to the dressing rooms, before smoothing her hair around her face and lifting her chin high. 'I guess I'll just have to move on then, won't I?'

'Good idea. Can I get you anything to make you feel better?'

'No. I'll get go and chill for a bit. Do my make-up. Get ready for the performance tonight.'

'Great idea.' Clio felt a leap of excitement. With Kylie out of the way she was safe to explore her and Dexter's dressing rooms. 'I hope you feel better soon.'

'Better?' Kylie's face hardened. 'I'm not going to waste any more time on Dex.' She shook her head. 'He's dead to me.' Then she turned and strutted through the door.

Clio texted the Mistletoe Murder Club WhatsApp chat and updated them on what she had learnt. Then, once Kylie had changed and walked out into the scrum of reporters, Clio went backstage to search Dexter's dressing room.

22

JEANIE

It was quite hard to do any kind of research while attempting to make gingerbread tree decorations with your children, but Jeanie was giving it her best shot. She had taken the baking slot to mollify her husband, Tan, who was less than impressed that she was now going to be out every night for the rest of the week, playing a pantomime cow. As Jeanie was less than impressed herself, she had struggled to know how to justify it, and the two of them had ended up having yet another argument while the children overdosed on *Bluey* in the front room. Happy bloody Christmas.

'Watch your fingers!' Jeanie put her phone down and leant over to help Yumi to press the Christmas tree cookie cutter into the small square of gingerbread dough that had survived the children's determined snacking. She wiped a smudge of flour from her daughter's cheek, feeling proud that they were doing such a festive family activity. Then she saw Jack launching a ball of dough at his twin's head, using her screams as a cover for him to attack the pile of presents under the Christmas tree. Back at the beginning of December she and Tan had truly believed that by placing the small tree on the table, they would mitigate the risk of it being knocked over. However, while this had worked well when the children were babies and incapable of movement, now it appeared naïve at best and foolish at worst. There was absolutely no way the tree wasn't going to come tumbling down soon, probably crushing all Jeanie's carefully chosen gifts for her children as it did so.

Jeanie loved Christmas, in theory. She loved buying presents for other people and opening the ones given to her. She loved the Christmas scents of cinnamon and cloves and mulled wine, loved the freezing air on her cheeks when she went out, loved the cosy warmth as she got home. She even loved the twins' feverish excitement as the big day approached. What she didn't love was having a murder investigation starting just as the festivities began, or having to play the back end of a cow in the pantomime.

Now, as she ushered Jack away from the presents, mollifying him with a cookie cutter shaped like a rocket ship – his current obsession was space and the planets – her mind snagged on the problem she had uncovered earlier, when she was piling up Beatrice Butler's diaries, ready for her to read and sift through for clues.

It was going to take a while. The pile of black notebooks was nearly as tall as Jeanie, each one labelled neatly in Beatrice's copperplate handwriting. But two years were missing. This year. And 1975. And Jeanie couldn't help wanting to know what they said.

This year's diary must still be at Beatrice's apartment, Jeanie thought. Maybe the 1975 diary was too.

The kids finished cutting their cookies and a strange array of gingerbread shapes lay on the baking trays, ready for Jeanie to put into the oven. She swallowed down a pang of guilt and then sent them into the living room to watch TV again. She needed to work out how to get into Beatrice's apartment and find the missing diary. She had a feeling that it might hold the key to working out who had carried out the murder.

Jeanie dug her laptop out from underneath a pile of picture books, and Googled *Beatrice Butler house*. An image appeared, linked into one of the many articles about her death and Jeanie instantly recognised the building. It was a luxurious apartment building with an uninterrupted view of the sea. Beatrice had moved in there with her late husband back in 2010 and had the penthouse apartment on the top floor.

Jeanie scrolled down and learnt that the building had a concierge. She messaged the Mistletoe Murder Club chat.

> Anyone know the concierge in Beatrice's building?

Almost before she'd finished typing, a reply pinged back.

MELISSA

Sure. He's called Carl. Likes licorice, the weirdo. He tried to share some when I was interviewing him for a job at the hotel. He didn't quite cut it at interview. Kept talking about Beatrice Butler, like dealing with her was some kind of qualification. I mean, sure, she was a diva, but...

JEANIE

Thanks. Will go get some liquorice!

MELISSA

Am I a detective now?

Jeanie grinned.

JEANIE

YES.

AMBER

NO.

MELISSA

How's that hottie Marco?

Everyone was typing now.

Clio's reply was a spewing face, Amber's a horrified face, Jeanie's a laughing face.

MELISSA

Ladies, I run a luxury hotel. I know quality when I see it.

Jeanie grinned and dialled Clio. Her friend picked up quickly.

'Hello? God, Melissa must be mad. I mean, Marco?!?'

'I know. Are you okay, Clio?'

'Why?'

Jeanie blinked. 'You're whispering.'

'Oh yes, so I am. I'm in Dexter's dressing room having a look around.'

'Oh. Okay.'

'No, it isn't okay, because the man is a walking dustbin.' Clio spoke in a hoarse whisper. 'It's disgusting in here. I'm not sure I'm going to get out alive.'

'Just hold your nose.'

'I can't.' Clio tutted impatiently. 'I told you, I'm rooting through his stuff. I need both hands for that.'

'Have you found anything interesting?'

'Nothing so far.' Clio sighed. 'But I've still got a fair few things to look through. He seems to have a lot of shoes, meaning a lot of boxes. Why did you call?'

'I'm reading through Beatrice's old diaries. And there's a gap. 1975 is missing. Do you know if she did anything different around then?'

'No idea.' Jeanie could hear the thud of boxes from Clio's end.

'It's just odd. All the rest are there, in order. Did you drop it, maybe, when you were piling them up in your caravan?'

'No.' Clio squealed. 'God these trainers smell disgusting. They're radioactive or something. No, all the diaries Jaxon gave me are there.'

'I wonder what happened in 1975?' Jeanie asked Google what productions Beatrice Butler had been in that year and came up with a blank. 'Maybe she took a year off?'

'Unlikely to have been by choice, if she did. I'd better go.' Clio cut the call.

Jeanie hoped she was okay. After checking on the twins, Jeanie got up and dialled Tan. He needed to get back here. Jeanie had places to be.

Half an hour later she was at Beatrice's building, offering Carl the doorman a Liquorice Allsort and her most charming smile. 'Thank you very much.' He patted his belly. 'They're my favourite.'

'Mine too,' lied Jeanie. 'How are you doing?'

'Not too great.' Carl shrugged his narrow shoulders. 'We lost one of our residents yesterday.'

'Beatrice Butler?'

'How did you know?'

Jeanie felt bad lying to him, but she had no choice. 'I'm her biographer – I'm working with Jaxon.' She took a gamble that he would have come round to work with Beatrice, or to collect the diaries.

She exhaled when Carl nodded. 'A sad job you've got there.'

Jeanie nodded. 'I know. But I want to do her memory proud.'

'Of course.'

'I – left something in her apartment. Might it be okay to go up there?' His brow lowered and she spoke in a rush. 'It's one of her diaries. Vital for the section I'm working on. I just want to get it right, you know?'

He smiled kindly, but shook his head. 'No. No one's allowed up, I'm afraid. The police have sealed it off.'

'Oh.' Jeanie's shoulders sagged. She had been so sure that diary would reveal something useful.

'I can tell you what happened yesterday morning though.'

'What's that?' Jeanie looked up, without much hope.

'Well, I saw someone try to run Beatrice over.'

'What?'

'Someone in a car accelerated towards her along the pavement, and came very close to knocking her over.' His kindly face turned serious. 'I ran out, of course, once I saw what had happened, but I was too busy seeing if she was okay to remember to take down the registration number. I could kick myself, I really could.'

'Did you see the driver at all?'

'Not really. All I could tell you is that it was a woman.'

'A woman?'

'Yes. But not the one on the news. Curlier hair, beneath a beanie or something. And a black car.'

Jeanie's mind whirled. 'I'm sorry you had to see that.' She smiled reassuringly. 'Thank you for telling me about it.'

'You're welcome.' He nodded. 'You seem kind. Easy to talk to. I told the police, but I think they thought I was seeing things. They didn't seem to take it seriously.'

'Then I'm glad you told me too.' Jeanie was about to shake his hand when her phone rang.

'Clio?'

'Help.'

'What?' Jeanie could barely hear her friend.

'Help.' This time the whisper was louder. 'Oh—' She went silent.

'Clio... Clio?'

'Someone's coming. I have to hide.'

'Clio?'

Then there was silence from the other end of the phone. Jeanie waited, pulse spiralling, hoping against hope that her friend would be okay. Then she waved goodbye to Carl and started to run.

23

BEATRICE BUTLER

16.25: Three hours until her death

Beatrice came out of the town hall well satisfied with her afternoon's work. The dress rehearsal had been significantly less appalling than the one the day before, and she had planted a few more seeds of discontent between Sylvia and Jaxon to ensure that the final element of her plan came together onstage. Sure, people were out to stop her, people wanted to tear down the theatre that she loved, but Beatrice was ahead of them. Beatrice was going to win. She was not going to die until the future of the Beatrice Butler Theatre was assured.

'Beatrice!'

She was not expecting to see the figure waving at her from across the street. He was wearing a cable-knit jumper and a pleading expression. As Beatrice watched he sprinted across the road, and she saw that he was carrying some flowers.

'Hello, Gawain.'

His smile was too eager. It reminded her of someone, but she couldn't quite place who.

'Are you heading back to the theatre, Beatrice?'

'Yes. I am.' She hoped she wouldn't have to walk the whole way with him. He had worked at the theatre for years, and was generally extremely competent, if a bit too talkative at times. He liked to tell her about his childhood with his adopted parents, and she was never quite sure why she needed all this detail about what toys he had, or what part he played in the school nativity. She was a woman who had acted opposite Sir Ian McKellen – what interest could she possibly have in him playing a Wise Man on some sweaty school stage somewhere?

He was talking as they walked along, but Beatrice did her best to tune him out. The planning officer had been most helpful just now, and had rubber stamped the paperwork to make the Beatrice Butler Theatre a listed building. Marg had done her work well. But Beatrice knew that one more touch was needed. One more event to truly make the theatre impregnable. Immortal.

'And do you know what I found out, Beatrice?'

Beatrice wondered if she could keep ignoring him.

'Beatrice?'

'What?' Her tone was sharp, but Beatrice Butler didn't care. They were nearly at the theatre now. She could have a cup of Lapsang Souchong in her dressing room, plant the pistol in its planned position on the props table. Put her plan in action.

'Well...' His voice was husky, his face shiny with sweat. The man really should start washing his face properly. One of the things Beatrice had loved most about Florian was his exemplary presentation. This sweat reminded her of someone else. Of that evening back in 1975. The stairs leading up to the hotel suite.

She looked at Gawain again. Really looked. His brown eyes had a green fleck. She remembered that fleck. She had seen it before in the man who had taken her hand and led her to his bedroom. The man she had knowingly seduced. The man who had given her the role that had made her name go stellar. Jamie Byngham.

A creeping dread prickled her skin. No. It couldn't be.

She searched the face of her companion as shoppers weaved around the two of them, staggering along with heavy bags, one man with a sizeable Christmas tree balanced on his back. Gawain's eyes were strangely knowing and strangely familiar. How had she never noticed that nose, so long and straight, just like...

No. Beatrice absolutely did not have time to be thinking things like this. It didn't matter who Gawain looked like – what mattered was that Beatrice got to the theatre and carried out her plan. She would not be deflected. She would not deviate from her path.

Gawain had other ideas. He seemed to be holding her hand and his palm was predictably clammy. It was all she could do not to squeal as she tried to free herself.

He clung on. 'Beatrice, you see, I think that you're my...'

She could see tears forming in his eyes. She could see the need, the vulnerability.

And she knew she could not tolerate it. She would never be what he needed her to be. Best to cut this off now.

'Gawain. Whatever you think you know, you are wrong.' She used her most commanding Lady Macbeth tones. 'So stop. Now. You are embarrassing yourself.'

His face crumpled, as she had known it would. 'But... I think you are my mother, Beatrice.'

She held up a hand. Mother. That word. Something she had never ever wanted to be, never ever felt capable of. 'Stop that nonsense, now. It is a lie. It is all lies. I am nobody's mother.' She took a deep breath to steady herself. 'And I'd appreciate it if you never ever mention this again.'

'But why? I am your and Florian's son, Beatrice! What's wrong with that?'

Florian's son? If only. She drew herself up to her full height, right there next to a tacky shop which was blasting out a song telling everyone to step into Christmas.

'Because if I had a son he would be nothing like you.' She sneered, desperate to get him to go away, to leave her in peace. 'He would be tall, masterful, talented, he would be king of all he surveyed. You...' She eyed him up and down, seeing the weakness, the need, the open, wounded heart. 'You are nothing.'

Then she sped up and marched towards the theatre. Locked in her dressing room ten minutes later, she loaded the pistol. She dressed it with mistletoe and tinsel, so that it looked like the prop gun that would be used in the final showdown between Clio's henchman and Jack, and then tucked it into her pocket and marched to the backstage area.

At the props table, she looked smartly to right and left. No one was here.

Gawain hadn't followed her when she had left him on the pavement and Beatrice was sure that she was alone.

Quietly, she picked up the prop gun and laid her own pistol on the table. Now all she had to do was to sit back and let the fireworks begin.

24

AMBER

Amber was on her way to the theatre, alerted by Jeanie to Clio's situation, when a sleek black car drew up beside her. Amber took no notice, continuing to charge towards the theatre from the car park by the pier, grabbing only her rucksack in case she needed any tools to get into the dressing room where Clio was hiding.

She was racing along the pavement, when she became vaguely aware of someone calling her name. She looked at the car to see the tinted window had rolled down to reveal the immaculate hair and cashmere cardigan of her old acquaintance Marg Redfearn. Amber had texted Marg to find out a couple of details about the case, but had yet to hear anything back. Maybe this time she was going to get the crime scene forensics information in person.

Marg called through the window. 'Amber. A minute of your time, if you please.'

Amber shook her head, worried about her friend. 'I've got to go and help Clio.'

'It'll take two minutes.'

'No.'

The car door swung open. 'Amber, you know I do not process the word no. I have information that is pertinent to the case, and I can see your friend Jeanie rushing into the theatre now, so whatever drama you're involved in, you clearly have it covered.' Marg's eyes were bright above the forbidding black frames of her glasses. 'One minute of your time and then you can go and save your friend, with much better information at your fingertips. So how about you hurry along and get inside the car, yes?'

It wasn't a question and Amber gave in, hoping that Jeanie and Clio would be okay. She ducked down and climbed onto a spotless grey leather seat. She had never been into one of Marg's inner sanctums before. Even in her days on the force, with a police badge as her entry permit, she had never made it past the front door of Marg's chocolate box cottage down near the seafront. Roses burst from hanging baskets outside, and a surfboard was always propped up by the garage, a sign of Marg's status as the over-70s surfing champion of the south coast.

The door swung shut and Amber swallowed down a surge of panic. Marg wouldn't do anything to Amber, wouldn't drive her off to a remote warehouse and set her heavies to work. Would she? Marg was renowned throughout the Sunshine Sands criminal scene and was ruthless. But she had always helped Amber, with the two of them forming an informal alliance on various murder cases over the past couple of years. Amber inhaled. The car smelt of new leather and fresh shortbread and it was clear from the tray on the small table inside the limo that Marg frequently ate on the move.

She smiled at Amber and somehow it was more terrifying than her habitual dour expression. 'Would you like one?' She pushed the plate of shortbread towards Amber.

It was unlike Marg to be so hospitable and Amber was too worried to eat. 'No thanks.' She shook her head. 'What is it that you want, Marg?'

Marg snapped back. 'It's you who wants something.'

'It is?'

'Forensics information, I believe.' Marg's eyes glinted.

'Yes.' Amber kept thinking about Clio. She shook her head, trying to dislodge the thoughts. 'I did.'

'But before I give it to you...'

Amber watched her, unsurprised. There was always a deal to be done with Marg.

'Yes?'

'You may be aware that Beatrice Butler and I were friends.'

'I was. And I'm sorry for your loss.'

Marg waved her condolences away. Whoever she confided her real feelings in, it was never going to be Amber.

'I am the voice of the Giant in her production.'

'Oh yes.' Amber remembered seeing her name on the programme. 'A favour for a friend?'

'I did it for my grandchildren. They love hearing me booming round that beautiful old theatre.' A lightness spread across Marg's face. It disappeared as rapidly as it had come, to be replaced by her customary glare. 'And because we were friends, Beatrice came to me yesterday, asking me for help, much as you have done. There were two things. She asked me to scare off someone who was using a long-ago secret to force her to sign the theatre over to developers, so it could be demolished. And she requested some support persuading the Council planning committee to agree to make the theatre a listed building too.'

'What was the secret?'

'The secret?' Marg shook her head. 'Obviously I can't tell you that. Nice try, though.'

'Did you do as she asked?'

'I did. We went back a long way, you know. But I haven't dealt with the individual she was talking about yet.' Marg's lips pressed into a hard line. 'I was having him followed, prior to teaching him a lesson. And I am here to tell you that the police have arrested the wrong person for Beatrice's murder.'

'I know.'

'I had a feeling you would.' Marg folded her hands across her immaculately pressed black trousers. Her usual pearls were around her neck, above a white blouse and a purple cashmere cardigan. 'I know because I decided to have eyes on all of them, in the end. Because I worked out what Beatrice was up to. She didn't tell me everything, but then she never does.'

Amber frowned. 'What do you mean?'

'She was cooking up a plan of her own. To make sure the theatre was never demolished – that its listed status would never be questioned.'

'How?'

Marg flicked a crumb of shortbread from her perfectly creased trousers. 'Well...'

'Yes?'

'I discovered that one of the planning officers told her that a dramatic event on the stage of a listed theatrical building can cement its national treasure status.'

'So?'

'So.' Marg frowned. 'Beatrice Butler was dying. Of cancer. A very unpleasant business, of course, and one that she certainly didn't talk about to me. But I knew.'

Of course, Amber reflected. Marg always knew everything. She probably knew what toothpaste Amber used and about her secret addiction to Tunnock's Teacakes.

'So what was she planning?'

'Well.' Marg arched her eyebrows. 'She was planning for someone to be killed onstage.'

'You what?' Amber's mouth fell open in shock. 'Who?'

'Even I don't know that. But someone. She swapped her loaded pistol with the prop gun, only to be shot with it herself backstage.'

'Oh my God.' Amber tried to process this. 'Do you know who did it?'

'I do not. That's what you're for. But I don't think it was Winnie. The killing was too direct. Too face to face. Beatrice ran rings around her.' Marg sniffed dismissively. 'I have no idea how you can allow someone to take your house. That girl is pathetic.'

Amber did her best to ignore this. 'So. Who was the one trying to blackmail Beatrice?'

Marg checked her discreet silver watch. 'Ross. He's quite unpleasant apparently, once he takes his stage make-up off.'

'I bet he is.' Amber's mind was whirring. Ross. The pantomime dame. Trying to blackmail Beatrice? Really? She felt another pang of fear as she wondered whether it was him who was coming after Clio right now. She had to get going. 'We'll keep an eye on him, Marg.'

'Good.' Marg sipped her tea. 'Although Amber...' Her voice held a warning note.

'Yes?'

'His prints weren't on any of the items found at the crime scene. Whereas Dexter, Sylvia, Winnie and Gawain were all there. So it may be that her killer is actually someone else altogether. Just make sure you get them locked up for good, okay?'

'We'll do our best.'

'Good. Time for you to go now.' The door had swung open again. Amber took the unsubtle hint and exited the vehicle.

She was going to find Clio and then this Ross guy.

He had some questions to answer.

25

CLIO

Clio was petite enough to squeeze herself into very small spaces, but as she lay underneath the chaise-longue in Dexter's dressing room, she wondered whether she was small enough to ever get back out. She had dived under here at speed, after hearing Dexter approaching, only managing to secrete herself successfully as he had stopped to answer a call on his mobile phone.

He had marched into the dressing room, apparently not noticing the fact that Clio had moved the shoeboxes around when she was searching. His voice was loud, and his tone was panicked.

'Look.' He had sat down on the chaise-longue, which had instantly bent to his weight, the springs stopping only marginally above Clio's nose. 'I have the money. I do. I promise. I will pay you, okay?'

A sigh from Dexter, as Clio could hear words firing from whoever was on the other end of the call.

'I told you. I have something to sell. Something big.'

Clio stiffened. This could be the ruby ring. Dexter could be the one who had stolen it, and as such, he must have lied to the police. She hadn't found it in her search so far, but as he talked on, she noticed a hole in the cover of the chaise-longue above her head. She raised her hand to explore it further, but with the springs looming so close to her face, beneath Dexter's weight, she didn't quite have enough room to stick her fingers into the gap and explore. She lay, frustrated, eyeing the hole. It would be the perfect hiding place.

'I get that you don't believe me, and I know I said I'd get you the money tonight. But just give me a few more hours, yeah?' Dexter's left leg was jiggling up and down and Clio feared that any minute now he would stick his hand beneath the chaise-longue to check that his precious treasure was still there.

Powerless to move, she decided to close her eyes and pretend she was elsewhere, but her eyes flicked open seconds later, when something metallic landed on her face. It was all she could do not to scream. It sat on the bridge of her nose, heavy, round and most definitely precious. She had a sneeze coming but did her best to bite it back. She could not move. If she did the ring might slide over her cheeks and drop to the floor with a giveaway clang. She lay, as still as she could, her crossed eyes trained on the ring.

She wasn't remotely surprised that Dexter had stolen it. Given what she had just found on her search, she suspected that he had stolen all of the items that had gone missing during rehearsals, as Kylie had implied. All of the wallets and earrings and credit cards that people had lost had probably been taken by Dexter himself, to fund what was clearly a spiralling gambling habit. One of his shoeboxes had contained a stack of betting slips for horses that Clio would guess had not come first in their races.

Above her, Dexter gave a loud groan. 'For God's sake. What does a man have to do to get some breathing space?' He stopped as Clio heard the volume go up at the other end of the line. She wondered who Dexter owed money to, and almost felt sorry for him. The ring was staying in position, for now. The chaise-longue creaked above her.

'I told you, I just need someone to sell the ring and we're good. It's meant to be worth at least half a million.'

Another pause, during which Clio wished she was recording this conversation.

A groan from Dexter. 'Oh, you're killing me with this. I thought you'd know someone who could fence it for me.' The ruby ring was about to slide off Clio's face now. It couldn't fall. The man above her might have killed to get his hands on the ring and she didn't want to be next on his list. Suddenly, he got to his feet, pacing back and forth across the dressing room, his voice rising. 'Well, then we've got a problem, haven't we? Because I can't give you the ring, because you only want money. But all I have is the ring and no one to buy it off me. So we're a bit stuck, aren't we?' His tone was aggressive now, and Clio could imagine his chest expanding, his spare fist clenching, his brow furrowing as he said the words. His feet came to a halt, just by Clio's head.

'Nah. I'm not the one who killed her.' Dexter sounded genuinely shocked. 'Why would you say that? I just nicked the ring, didn't I? I saw an opportunity, and I took it.'

Another pause. Then Dexter exhaled sharply. 'That's not my problem.' His voice got quieter, more ominous. 'I've staked everything on this. I've sacrificed so much. I took the role in the crappy panto, surrounded by a talentless cast.'

Clio was itching to say something. She wasn't talentless. She had been an understudy in the original production of *Cats*. And also, what had he sacrificed? All he had done was steal everyone else's stuff and never learnt his lines. He was pretending he was the good guy here, that the world was doing him down, painting himself as some kind of martyr, gaslighting the rest of the cast. She was half-tempted to get out from under the chaise-longue and yell at him.

But she couldn't, because then he would know how much Clio had discovered. And, even though Clio considered herself extremely scrappy, she didn't know if she would come off that well in a fight.

It was as she was thinking this that the ring finally clanged to the floor.

Dexter spoke rapidly into the phone. 'Hang on. I'll call you back.'

He must have heard it fall. Clio froze, irrationally holding her breath to try to make herself smaller. As Dexter walked up to where the ring had landed she started spiralling. Please don't let him find her. Please. It was nearly Christmas. She wouldn't get to embarrass Nina by wearing her beloved Santa outfit. She wouldn't get to eat Bez's amazing turkey stuffing. No pigs in blankets! Clio felt like weeping.

She heard a click of a middle-aged knee bending and closed her eyes. The ring was just by her left hand. She was doomed. Dexter was going to find her. He was going to drag her out of her hiding place, and...

She heard footsteps at the door. Please let it be Jeanie or Amber. Please let them save her. She would never do anything stupid again. She wouldn't make them play the cow. She would behave. For ever.

The door opened. Clio held her breath.

'Who the hell are you?' There was a new wildness to Dexter's words, a rough edge to his voice. Clio listened, praying it was one of her friends. Maybe Dexter wasn't a joke, maybe he was a dangerous man who had been covering his tracks. Maybe beneath the tan and the teeth he would do absolutely anything to get what he needed to survive.

'Dexter!' Clio smelt floral fabric softener and felt a rush of affection. She would know that voice anywhere. Jeanie had come to find her, just as Clio had known she would. It was so good to have friends like her, friends who were family, who would run towards killers without a thought, who would do anything to save their friends.

'Dexter! I'm Jeanie, I'm just helping out backstage tonight. I'm so sorry to bother you but it's…' There was a pause, as Jeanie made something up. 'It's time to run through your lines.'

'Why?' Dexter sounded indignant. 'I know them perfectly.'

Liar. He was still writing them on his arm, for God's sake.

'The director wants a full run-through. Come on.' Jeanie was breathing fast. She'd clearly been running hard.

Clio grinned. Well done, Jeanie.

'But…'

'Now!' Jeanie's voice was full of an authority it normally lacked. 'Come on.'

Muttering, Dexter got to his feet and Clio breathed a sigh of relief as he walked out of the room.

After a moment, Jeanie's bright blue eyes were next to Clio.

'Are you okay?'

'I am. And look what I found.' Clio slid out from under the chaise-longue and gave Jeanie a big hug. As always, her friend smelt of apple shampoo and of home, always Clio's safe harbour in choppy seas. She held out the ring.

'Oh my God! He had it!'

Clio nodded. 'He did, the lying bastard.'

Amber appeared in the doorway. 'Oh, thank God you're okay, Clio. I ran all the way from Marg's car.'

'Why were you in that?'

'She wanted to tell me about Ross. He was trying to get Beatrice to sign something allowing the theatre to be demolished. But instead, she was aiming to get it listed.'

'Ross?' Clio felt a bitter pang of disappointment.

'Yes. He was trying to blackmail her into signing the deal to knock it down.' Amber smiled. 'But he clearly had no idea who he was dealing with. Beatrice ran rings round him, apparently.'

'Ross?' Clio blinked. 'Lovely, cuddly Ross? My pal?'

Amber nodded. 'Is an arsehole? Yes.'

Clio dropped her eyes to the carpet. 'But I really liked him!'

Amber rolled her eyes. 'Classic Clio. Your antennae are useless.'

'No, they're not!' Clio shook her head. 'Well, maybe a little bit.'

She swallowed her sense of betrayal and showed Amber the ring. 'Look, it was in here, so Dexter must have stolen it. But we still don't know who killed Beatrice.'

Amber nodded. 'Well, Marg told me that Sylvia, Gawain, Winnie and Dexter all left prints in Beatrice's dressing room, so it has to be one of them, doesn't it?'

Clio frowned. 'That's not a very narrow field, is it?'

'No.' Amber shook her head, visibly frustrated.

'Just as well you've got me then, isn't it?'

'Melissa?' Amber turned.

'The very same.' Melissa was dressed in a 'Fleece Navidad' jumper with a huge sheep on a red background and jeans. She was glowing with self-satisfaction. 'Guess who knows who set the light up to fall?'

'You?' Clio stepped forward eagerly. 'Who was it?'

'And how do you know?' Amber arched an eyebrow.

'Publicity photos, baby!' Melissa grinned. 'I only got a tiny shot of the corner of their leg, but it's enough, given the beautiful scarlet stockings they're wearing, isn't it?' She showed them a photo on her phone screen, and in the corner of the lighting rig, above the stage, where Dexter and Kylie were standing, was a shapely leg in a scarlet stocking.

The trio looked at each other. 'ROSS.'

'Oh my God, he tried to kill her.'

'So did someone else, outside her apartment!' Jeanie's voice squeaked out. 'A woman. With curly hair.'

'Kylie?'

The four of them stared at each other. 'Do you think everyone's had a go?'

Amber nodded. 'Maybe.'

They all stayed silent for a second, then Amber clapped her hands together. 'Of course. Marg just told me that was Beatrice's plan! That someone would try and kill someone onstage. That way, the theatre would become a listed building, and could never be knocked down.'

Clio gasped. 'But instead, they all turned on her?'

Amber nodded; her face serious. 'Well, we don't know that yet. We know that Winnie poisoned her drink, we suspect that Kylie tried to run her down in a car, we know that Dexter stole the ring, and we have photographic evidence that Ross was up on the lighting rig just before the spotlight fell. So, that's a poisoned mince pie, strangle marks and the gunshot wound to go.'

'Bloody hell.' Clio couldn't believe it. 'Am I the only one who didn't try to murder her?'

'Maybe.'

Clio grinned. 'Does that mean I'm officially a grown-up?'

The other three spoke in unison. 'No way.'

Melissa clapped her hands together. 'Shouldn't we tell the police? I could give Marco a call?'

Amber shook her head. 'No. We still don't know who the killer is. If we tell Marco now, he'll just arrest everyone and we'll never know.'

Melissa frowned. 'He can't be that stupid. He's so handsome.'

Amber rolled her eyes. 'I knew there was a reason you and Clio got along, Melissa. You both have terrible taste in men. And he's not handsome!'

Jeanie spoke in a whisper. 'There is one more thing.'

'Yes?'

'Well, I was going through her diaries, and I found a gap. In 1975. No diary and Beatrice wasn't in any shows either. Which was weird, because her career was just getting started. And then...' Jeanie pulled something out of her pocket. 'I found this pink piece of paper under one of the seats on the day Beatrice was killed.' She unfolded it. 'I only just realised what it was and looked it up on the way here. It's a hospital number, and a hospital name. The Mounthill hospital, near Scotland. And I think, if we get into the hospital records, that we'll find that Beatrice had a baby there.'

'Oh my GOD.' Clio blinked.

'You guys are dope.' Melissa's eyes were round. 'And this Mistletoe Murder Club is the best! Am I a member now? Am I? Am I? Sis?'

Amber shuddered. 'I told you. No "sis." NO.'

A bell rang again, and Clio realised with horror that it was the half-hour call.

'Um. Amber and Jeanie?'

'What?' Amber was trying to avoid her half-sister's embrace.

'Well, it's half an hour until the show starts?'

'WHAT?' Amber looked like she was about to flee.

'Just thought you might want to know.'

'Oh God.' Jeanie put her head into her hands. 'But we don't know who the killer is.'

Amber shook her head. 'Not to mention we don't know what Daisy the Cow actually does.'

Clio had to be the calm one. She was sure she could pull it off, just this once. 'Look we're going to have to keep trying to figure this out from backstage. Maybe Ross tried again? Maybe Dexter pulled the trigger? But see what you can figure out while the show is on, okay? And Melissa? Keep an eye on what's happening out front. See what you can see.'

'Got it.' Melissa gave a salute. 'Good luck out there, you three.' She trapped Amber in a hug just as she left the room. 'Take care, sis. I haven't annoyed you enough yet. This is not the time to die.'

'I don't even know where the costume is.' Amber sighed.

'I'll show you.' Clio led the way out of the room, the ring still in her pocket 'Now, let's get out there and put on a show.'

'Um. Okay.' Jeanie swallowed. 'Here we go. My adult stage debut.'

'And our chance to catch a killer.' Amber swallowed. 'Let's do this.'

ACT THREE

HE'S BEHIND YOU

26

JEANIE

As a woman with absolutely no stage ambitions whatsoever, Jeanie would not have felt particularly comfortable putting on the back end of a cow costume, even if there hadn't been a killer on the loose in the building.

'Who's the stage manager, as Winnie isn't here?' She pulled on one leg of the costume. 'Because they're going to have a lot of work to do to get us in the right place.'

Clio pulled a face. 'I've just heard that it's going to be Gawain.'

'The one person we haven't talked to?'

'Yes.' Clio nodded. 'The one who was weeping by the body when we found it.' She sucked air in through her teeth as she layered on her green make-up. 'I keep wondering about the long-lost child thing. Could it be Sylvia? She seems a bit young. Or Jaxon, maybe? He's around fifty, isn't he?'

Amber looked dubiously at Daisy's head, hoping it smelt less garlicky now. She groped inside it and the eyelids started to bat up and down as she pulled a tiny string inside the cow's cheek. 'That's going to have to be my party trick.' She gritted her teeth. 'If I just keep doing this the whole way through the show no one will notice that we're in the wrong place or that we don't know any of the dances.'

She stuck her head out of Clio's dressing room, scoping the corridor, before darting back inside. 'So all we have to do is get someone to confess, yes?'

Jeanie inserted one leg into the costume. 'Exactly. And how are we going to do that?'

'Well, we'll point out that you've got the ruby ring, Clio, and go from there. Hopefully, that will get the killer angry enough to reveal themselves.'

'Um. Okay.' Clio pulled a face. 'As long as you two will protect me from them. Dexter seems pretty desperate right now and he won't be happy with me.'

'Of course.' Amber nodded. 'And I know the plan isn't exactly foolproof, but it's all we've got, isn't it?'

Jaxon burst into the room, dressed in a purple shirt and a sharp black suit. 'Showtime. Gawain's bloody vanished, taking the stage manager headset with him, so I'm here in person to tell you it's time to get to the stage.' He surveyed Amber and Jeanie, who were half inside the cow costume now. 'So, are you two ready to get your Daisy on?'

'Absolutely not.' Amber shook her head. 'Any tips?'

Jaxon pushed his pork-pie hat further back on his head. 'Follow Jack. And whenever you hear music starting, dance.'

'Dance?' Amber looked at the cow's head in her hand, complete with bright red lips and huge green eyes. 'I don't dance in real life, let alone when I'm wearing a cow costume. I'll pass on that, thanks.'

'Then the little children who are here for their big Christmas night out won't laugh.' Jaxon folded his arms, frowning severely. 'And they might get upset and throw their Haribo at you. Do you want that? Do you want to take away the joy of the little children?' His voice hardened. 'Do you?'

Amber blinked. 'Um. No?'

'Well, obviously you don't.' He shook his head. 'It's Christmas, so just dance, okay?'

'But...'

'For the children?'

Amber subsided. 'OK then.'

Jeanie thought about Jaxon's prints in Beatrice's dressing room and about the woman who had said she hated Beatrice. She wanted to find out who it had been and now might be her last chance.

She looked at Jaxon, snapping her cow leg braces up over her shoulders and taking a punt. 'Why was Sylvia in Beatrice's dressing room before she was killed?'

Instantly, Jaxon's eyes began to dart around the room. 'What?'

Jeanie continued, sounding as confident as she could. 'I heard her, telling Beatrice Butler that she hated her.'

'Oh, I...' He stopped. 'Was that Sylvia? I didn't know she was in there. I wasn't around.'

'No?' Jeanie smiled sweetly. 'That's strange, because your fingerprints are in the dressing room. Did you know that?'

'Of course he bloody knew that.' Sylvia appeared in the doorway, her blonde hair twisted into a bun on top of her head, her entire body covered in glitter, the silver dress sweeping to the floor. 'Don't make stuff up, Jaxon.'

She turned to Jeanie. 'We were both in her dressing room. Just trying to get her to see sense, you know?'

'How?'

'Oh. Persuasion, of course.' Sylvia smiled. 'She was going to get me a job on a movie. Some old contact or other. But she was being a bit slow. Like with your book, too, Jaxon darling. She was a bit slow with that too, wasn't she? Not really a helper, Beatrice, was she? And it was the perfect opening for me – my big break – a drama set during the French revolution, set to a rap soundtrack. So much scope for colour, texture, you know.' Her blue eyes burned with an energy that bordered on fanatical.

'Um. Yes.' A muscle flickered in Jaxon's cheek. 'Beatrice was being slow.' He made as if to leave the room. 'But fun though it is discussing this, it's not really getting us in panto mood, is it?'

A voice came over the Tannoy and Gawain's Welsh accent rang out.

'Five minutes until curtain up. Beginners to the stage please.'

'Oh, he's back.' Jaxon looked relieved.

Amber looked round at Jeanie. 'Are we beginners?'

Jeanie smiled, her mind still whirring. 'It certainly feels like it.'

Jeanie bent forwards and grasped Amber's waist as Clio zipped the costume together. 'Come on, Daisy.' She opened the door and Jeanie started to shuffle towards the stage. Clio directed them forwards, telling them about steps and turns, and directing them to stop when they reached the side of the stage. Then, Amber suddenly halted and Jeanie barrelled straight into the back of her.

'What is it?'

Clio's voice was tiny. 'We have a problem.'

Amber sounded muffled. 'A bigger problem than knowing absolutely nothing about what the hell we're meant to be doing in this show?'

'A bigger problem even than that.'

'OK, what is it?' Jeanie felt her pulse spiral.

Clio's sounded like she was struggling to breathe. 'Well, it's mainly that Ross is standing in our way.'

'OK, well ask him to move.'

'And he has a knife.'

'WHAT?'

Amber spoke through gritted teeth. 'I was about to tell you not to overreact, but it's a little late for that.'

'Sorry.' Jeanie's throat was dry. 'What does he want?'

Clio squeaked out a reply. 'I don't know. But he's pointing the knife at your throat, Amber.'

'OK.' Jeanie whispered. 'Do you have any kind of plan, Amber?'

'Not yet.' Amber's voice was slow and calm. The kind of voice you use when you've been in the police force for decades and you're used to getting out of difficult situations. 'But I'm working on it.'

Then Jeanie heard Ross's voice. 'Stop right there. I know that you've got evidence that I was up on the lighting rig. And I'm here to tell you that there's no way I'm going to let you share it with anyone. Not now, and not ever.'

27

CLIO

It was the first time Clio had seen a pantomime dame bearing a knife. Fake pistols, yes, custard pies, yes, but never a knife, and certainly never holding a pantomime cow hostage. She felt fury and terror competing for space inside her. She had given Ross snacks, listened as he banged on about the houses he had for sale, spent hours at The Ovation with him.

'I saw Melissa's publicity shots.' He spoke through gritted teeth, his once affable expression replaced by one of pure rage. 'She put them online earlier and there I was, in the corner.'

'Oh no.' Clio saw the metal of the knife pressing against Amber's black and white spotted neck and swallowed. She really thought he might hurt her. He had tried to kill Beatrice, after all. This man was capable of anything.

Clio forced herself to speak. 'So what are you planning now, Ross?'

She could see Amber and Jeanie trying to disentangle themselves from the cow costume.

'Stop that.' Daisy stopped moving. The blade was long and threatening in his hand. Clio could see the hoops of his Dame corset digging into the furry legs. He was shaking, every inch of him taut.

She spoke before she could stop herself. 'Ross. Are you alright?'

'Don't you try and sweet-talk me, Clio.' There were tears in his voice.

'Ross. I'm not sweet-talking you. We're friends. Aren't we?' Clio was following instinct. What else could you do when there was a knife being pointed at your best friend's throat? 'And – this isn't like you.'

'You have no idea what I'm really like.'

Amber was moving inside the costume again, more subtly this time. Clio needed to distract Ross, hoping that would enable her friend to liberate herself.

His red heart lips pursed in distress. 'I don't want to hurt your friend, but I will if I have to.'

'But why?'

'Because I'm in too deep.' His voice broke. 'I'm a fixer for this local development firm. And they paid me a lot of money to get Beatrice to sign the agreement to knock down the theatre. You know what I'm like, I always say I can do things, I've always been an optimist. You know that. It's one of my biggest flaws.'

'That's true.' Even though he was holding Amber at knifepoint, even though he had tried to kill Beatrice, Clio felt a swell of sympathy for this man. 'But, maybe hurting Amber won't really help? Maybe...'

He wiped the sweat off his brow. 'Shut up.'

Clio did so, closing her eyes as if in prayer. There was a rush of footsteps coming towards her, and she was sure this was the end, was sure that he would slice Amber's neck any moment now. She thought of the three of them, laughing in Clio's beach hut, drinking margaritas and massacring 'Mamma Mia' on Clio's ancient karaoke machine.

Then a hand pulled her forwards, and she opened her eyes to see Amber, tall and fearless, holding the knife in her hand and a pair of handcuffs in the other. Still in her cow leggings, she snapped the cuffs onto him, imprisoning his hands together behind his back. 'That's quite enough of that, thank you.'

'Let me out of these things!' Spit flew from Ross's lips, the anger of his words such a mismatch with his Pantomime Dame costume that it almost made Clio laugh. 'I'm just a man trying to get by, you can't assault me like this!'

Clio shook her head. 'You tried to kill someone, Ross. You just held Amber hostage! And you tried to blackmail Beatrice. Who even are you?'

His eyes flashed fire. 'It's all bloody Beatrice's fault. If she had only signed over the theatre, like anyone sensible would have done, then I wouldn't have had to do all those things, would I?' His fake boobs nearly fell off as his thrashing about got wilder and wilder. 'And the big boys were after me, telling me I needed to get this job done, to persuade her. And I tried everything I could to do it. I tried logic, I tried passion, I tried blackmail.'

He exhaled loudly. 'Nothing worked. Nothing at all. And the developers were breathing down my neck.' He looked downwards, his false eyelashes fluttering. 'And I'm not proud of this, but I knew I had to do something about it all, to move things forwards, you know? And yesterday someone came and smashed the front window at my house, and I knew it was them. So, I...' He stopped. 'I had no choice. I went up to the lighting rig. I just wanted to scare her I guess, not to really kill her. I was relieved when it missed, to be honest.' He looked up, his eyes almost pleading beneath his extravagant Pantomime Dame lashes. 'That's why I kept making jokes, Clio. I'm not a killer, not really.' He dropped his head. 'When she was really killed – and I promise you it wasn't me – I was gutted. And I was freaking out that everyone would think it was me – if Beatrice had told anyone about what I was trying to get her to do.'

'She did tell someone.' Amber watched him, arms folded. Clio wondered how many times her friend had listened to criminals giving speeches like this – trying to justify what they had done.

Amber focused back on Ross, her eyes lasers. 'Listen.'

'Yes?'

'You say you didn't kill her.'

'I didn't.'

'Then why on earth did you claim that you did? Clio heard you on the phone, taking all the credit.'

'Oh God. That.' Sweat patches were blooming in his pale blue silk costume. 'I needed to pretend to the developers that I'd done it. So I'd get paid.'

'Ross!' Clio shook her head. 'That's terrible.'

'No. It's survival.'

'And we heard you on the pier too, saying the same thing.'

'Yeah.' Ross sighed. 'That was the boss man. I was in too deep by then. Nothing I could do but try to keep swimming. I even got some latex gloves and went and wrote a message in her dressing room, in her lipstick, to try to scare her. Nothing doing. She was made of iron.'

Amber frowned. 'So where were you when she was killed?'

'In my dressing room, trying to work out what the hell to do.'

'Any witnesses?'

'No.' He fiddled with his wig, which matched his infamous stockings. 'No one.'

His voice was rising, and they were joined by Dexter, Sylvia and Jaxon. With the fire curtain down, cutting the stage off from the audience, Clio hoped the audience wouldn't be able to hear them.

'Who's got it, then?' Dexter was in his first costume, pointy black shoes with large silver buckles and the blue Prince Charming frock coat. His face, however, didn't match his outfit. Veins stood out in his neck and his skin was a mottled red, even through his thick stage make-up.

'Who's got what?' Kylie had appeared now, in her urchin's costume as Jack, with ragged trousers with purple stripes to match Daisy the Cow's purple spots.

Dexter turned on her. 'I bet it was you!'

Kylie blinked. 'What was me?'

'I bet you've got it.'

'Got what?' Kylie took a step towards him, her face scrunching up in rage.

'Got the ring! You've stolen it! You're trying to ruin me.'

'Oh shut up, Dexter. Why does everything always have to be about you?'

'Piss off.' Dexter was closing in on Kylie.

'Oh, grow up, you loser.' Ross was getting angry now, even from his handcuffed position on the floor. The ability of men to compete with each other, when there was absolutely no point doing so, had always amazed Clio. Someone was dead, they still didn't know who the killer was, and yet these two were busy playing apex predator.

Dexter stared at Ross. 'Why am I the loser, when you're the one in handcuffs?'

They didn't have time for this. 'Look. We have an audience out there and a show to do. Can you two stop preening and get on with it?' Clio commanded.

'Calm down, darling.' Dexter laid a patronising hand on her shoulder. 'I just need Kylie to give me the ring, and…'

'The ring!' Clio batted his hand away. 'I knew it was you.'

Amber grabbed Dexter by the arm, twisting his forearm up behind him. 'Why *did* you take Beatrice's ruby ring, then, Dexter?'

He froze. 'Um. I…' He clearly hadn't realised how much he had given away. 'I…' He collected himself. 'I didn't. I was covering for Kylie.'

'You bastard.' Kylie attacked him, beating at his chest with her fists.

Clio rolled her eyes. These people. So dramatic. 'Dexter, I heard you on the phone. I know you're in debt. I know you took the ring. I heard you confessing.'

'What?' He swung round, her childhood crush becoming just another selfish, arrogant man who thought the world owed him a living. 'That's trespass.'

'No.' Amber's voice cut across him. 'It's really not. It's called hiding from a potential killer. Not illegal. In fact, very sensible indeed. So back off.' She squared up to him, standing deliberately in front of Clio.

'But...'

Amber shook her head. 'No. Back the hell off.'

He did so, muttering to himself, and then began arguing with Kylie again in the kind of whispers that could probably be heard in the front row of the stalls.

Clio drew Amber and Jeanie aside.

'What are we going to do with them?'

Amber frowned. 'Well, Ross can't go onstage, so I think we'll have to stop the show. And we need to get the police down here for Kylie, Dexter and Ross. Ross definitely tried to extort, blackmail and kill Beatrice, while Kylie may well have done the same, and Dexter definitely stole her ring.'

'Do you want to make the call, Amber?'

'Sure.' Amber patted her pocket, before remembering she was in costume. 'Damn. Do either of you have a phone?'

Clio gestured to her shapeless sack. 'No.'

'Jeanie?'

Jeanie shook her head as she frantically massaged her neck. 'Sorry. No room to stash anything inside that costume.'

'Right.' Clio made a decision. She drew Jeanie and Amber close, so no one else could hear them. 'Amber, you stay here and keep an eye on this lot, and I'll go and get a phone. The killer is still on the loose, and I, for one, don't want to put the audience at risk. I'll go and call the police and then go and find Gawain and see what he has to say for himself.'

It was at that very moment that an announcement came over the Tannoy.

'Ladies and gentlemen, I am sorry to say that this evening's performance has been cancelled, and we need to evacuate the building urgently.'

Clio blinked at her friends. 'Is that Gawain? He sounds different.' They could hear an instant swell of panicky chatter from the audience, followed rapidly by the creaking of seats and the rustle of sweet packets being stuffed into handbags. Children squealed as they were presumably dragged out by their parents, and footsteps thundered towards the door.

Clio took a deep breath, trying to steady herself. Getting the audience out was a good thing. Now at least the public weren't in danger.

Amber spoke in a low voice. 'Melissa had better get the hell out of there. I hope she doesn't get any stupid ideas in her head about leaping in to save us.'

Clio saw the fear on her friend's face. Melissa had broken her way in to Amber's heart, it seemed. She felt a pulse of joy, rapidly followed by fear as a siren wailed throughout the theatre.

'Please be as quick as you can.' A siren began to sound, high-pitched and painful. 'There has been another murder. Everyone must evacuate.'

Clio gasped.

'What?'

Gawain spoke again. 'I repeat. There has been another murder. Please evacuate the building as quickly as you can.'

'What?' Ross somehow managed to get to his feet, staggering in his ridiculous high heels, his fake boobs bobbing in front of him. 'Let me out. I don't want to die. I have so much to give. Let me out of these handcuffs!'

Only Amber remained still. 'Who has been murdered? Everyone's here.'

'What?' Clio ran to the fire curtain, trying to shift it but it wouldn't budge. She ran to the door that led back towards the dressing rooms. It was also locked.

'Oh my God, we're trapped!'

Amber shook her head. 'Gawain. He wants us all together. He wants us all back here.'

Clio took Jeanie's hand. Her friend was trembling and frankly, Clio thought she had good reason. 'So? What do we do now?'

'Look.' Amber shook her head as Dexter and Kylie ran around the stage, screaming that all the doors had been locked. 'Gawain is playing a game here. He is terrifying us all, and he's trapped us here. He wants us to be scared. He wants us to panic.'

'What do we do, Amber? What do we do?'

And then the lights went out and they were plunged into darkness so thick that the only thing Clio could make out was the sound of her own breathing as she waited for whatever horrors Gawain had in store.

28

BEATRICE BUTLER

18.45: Forty minutes until her death

Beatrice walked over and put the flaming 1975 diary into the sink. Burning it was the only way to keep her secret hidden for good, now Gawain and Ross were sniffing around. She watched the flames rising until she was absolutely sure that no one could learn anything from its charred remains.

She picked the blackened remnants of the diary out of the sink and threw them into the bin. Then she opened her cuttings book, flicking back to the golden days of her early career. Cleopatra at the Wyndham's, Portia at the Edinburgh Festival, opposite Mark Rylance, and on and on. Back then life had seemed so simple. She and Florian forever, role after role landing in her lap, due, in part, to his money and influence.

They had agreed early never to have children. As she leafed through the book, seeing her young face shining out of black and white pictures accompanied by glowing reviews from all the major nationals, she remembered the magic of those times, the way she had believed that the roles would never run out, that she would be the toast of the West End forever. The night she had won her Olivier, she and Florian had toasted each other, congratulating themselves on how very lucky they were.

And the next day she had auditioned for a role in *Les Liaisons Dangereuses* and her whole world had changed in the very worst of ways. Beatrice remembered that terrible day when she realised that the weight she had been gaining had not been due to overconsumption of the petits fours that Florian had brought back from Paris, but instead the residue of her one illicit night with the *Les Liaisons* director, Jamie Byngham. He was a tall man, with curly brown hair and a suggestive smile. When he had asked to meet Beatrice for dinner, she hadn't thought much about it. Florian was away on a shooting trip, as was his wont, and so Beatrice had accepted Jamie's invitation. But then one thing had led to another, canapés and champagne becoming a shared soufflé, becoming cocktails and then whisky up in his hotel suite.

Beatrice had sat there on a very expensive sofa and remembered little Betty, who felt lucky if she got ten pence to buy sweets once a month. She gazed up at the chandelier, ran a hand over the thick velvet sofa and then glanced down at the heavy crystal glass on the low coffee table in front of her. Life with Florian was luxurious, of course, but it had also somehow become tame. Predictable. Tonight, she felt a spark of danger in the air, and it excited her.

Jamie sat next to her on the sofa, the distance between them no more than a few centimetres. And then he leant closer and kissed her. And Beatrice had let him, had started kissing him back. But then, three months later, the penny had dropped. She had been forced to face the prospect of becoming a mother and ruining everything she and Florian had. She couldn't let Florian know the truth, and so she had lied and covered up the lie again and again until she had believed she was safe.

She had been too late to get rid of the baby – too late to do anything but work out how to cover it all up. She had told Florian that she was pregnant, of course, but she had made him believe that the baby was his, just as she had made him see that they could not possibly keep it. It would be too much, it would hold them back, it would end Beatrice's career. Even when the baby was born, far away in a Scottish hospital, they had remained resolute. She had handed it over to the nurse straight away, ready for its adoptive parents to take it, and love it, without even looking at the mewling, squalling little thing. She had felt nothing but relief as the door had closed behind her child.

She turned the page with shaking fingers, seeing the year-long gap between the playbills featuring her name. The baby was born in between her appearance in *Les Liaisons Dangereuses* and her bravura turn as Cathy in the National Theatre's stage production of *Wuthering Heights*. The critics had said she was too skinny for the role, which Beatrice had only ever taken as a compliment, given that she had given birth only months before.

She ran a finger over the picture of her face beneath the wild, dark wig she had worn as Cathy. She looked strong, brave, defiant. Magnificent, even. A woman to be reckoned with. She felt a surge of pride. She hadn't let a child ruin her life. She had followed through, given it away, and never looked back. She raised her eyes to the mirror, seeing a woman who was still fighting. Still here.

Now, the knock came again, and Beatrice knew who it would be. She was so tired of running. So tired of pretending. She wanted to take off her mask and speak the truth, before it was too late, even if the person listening didn't want to hear what she had to say. He needed to move on too, to stop chasing a mother who had never wanted him, to stop yearning for a happy ending that would never ever happen.

'Come in.' She turned to face him, head held high, ruby ring sparkling on her finger.

The door opened and Gawain came in. Those eyes, so like Jamie's. That sweaty skin, the thinning hair. Could this really be her son? It was enough to make her shudder.

'Beatrice. We need to talk.'

'No.' She shook her head. 'We don't.'

'Oh, I think we do.' He walked towards her, and she stood, head back, summoning every inch of her theatrical poise.

'For once, Mother, you don't get to call the shots.'

The use of 'Mother' threw her. She had never wanted to be a mum. Florian had given her all the love she had ever wanted.

She wanted Gawain out of here. She was angry with him for finding her, angry with him for disrupting her pre-show routine.

'What do you want, Gawain?'

'Beatrice, I'm just asking you to listen to me. Please. Just listen. Why won't you ever listen to me?'

'Why on earth would I listen to you?'

'Oh, I don't know.' He threw his arms wide. He was normally so submissive that it was a shock to see him marching around the room, picking up her precious things and putting them down again. 'Maybe because I'm your child? And maybe, as your child, I might expect some love? Maybe some maternal care? I don't know. What do mums normally give their kids?'

This was ridiculous. 'You're not my child. I gave you away. You went to a good home.'

Gawain swung round, his face twisted. 'I *am* your child. You just chose to reject me.'

He was taller than her. Wider than her. Beatrice hesitated. Surely he wouldn't really hurt her? No.

'Get out, Gawain.' She pointed her finger at the door.

'No.'

She faltered. He was close now. So close she could see the open pores on his nose and smell the pickle on his breath.

'Get. Out.'

'No.' His hands closed around her neck and squeezed.

And the world began to blur as Beatrice Butler staggered, fought and then went still.

29

CLIO

When productions went dark, it was normally after the first night, when the critics had savaged the actors, the set, the music, the script and when ticket sales were barely more than zero. But this production seemed to be moving at speed. Clio held her hands out in front of her, flinching as they encountered a backside that she could not identify. She rapidly withdrew them and turned away.

'Who's there?' She dropped her hands to her sides again.

'Jeanie.' Her friend's voice was high and tense. 'It's Jeanie.'

'Oh good.' Clio reached out and took her hand. 'Let's stick together, okay?'

'Me too.' Amber was on her other side. 'Stay quiet.' Amber dropped her voice still lower. 'Are you sure neither of you have a phone?'

'No, we don't.' Clio shook her head, realising as she did so that Amber couldn't see her.

Dexter's voice came from their left, quite a long way away, as if he were on the other side of the stage already. 'Let us out of here!'

Jeanie gave a squeal of fear. 'God, this is awful. If we make it through this, I am never ever going onstage again.'

'Me neither.' Clio could almost hear Amber's mind whirring, figuring out how to escape. 'I wonder what he's planning?'

'I dread to think.' Clio wondered if they could somehow clamber up the long ladder that led up to the lighting bar or the flies, but knew it was too risky in the dark.

'We could use the trapdoor?'

'Oh yes!' Amber nodded. 'Where is it?'

Clio tried to slow her breathing and orientate herself but couldn't manage it. 'Um. That way?' She pointed vaguely into the middle distance.

'Can't see you, Clio.'

'Sorry. Follow me.' Gingerly she started to lead her friends across the stage, finding herself ducking back and flinching at every unknown sound. Where the hell was Gawain and what was he trying to prove? They could only hope that one of the audience would do the sensible thing and dial 999, that someone would appear soon to try to help them. She squeezed Jeanie's fingers. 'I think it's here. Ow.' She had only succeeded in bumping into a piece of scenery. She put her hand to her face. 'God, that hurt.'

Beside her, she could feel Amber's frustration. 'We need a plan. We can't just wander around until he turns the lights back on.' Clio could hear Dexter, Kylie and Ross committing to some serious panicking to the right of the stage. They were crashing around, hitting the scenery, which emitted hollow metallic clanging noises and then loud wooden bangs. Then they moved and sounded like they were approaching Clio and her friends, before one of them tripped and fell, swearing, to the stage.

Amber tutted. 'Those three aren't going to be any use. Any ideas on what we can do? Can we get hold of Jaxon and Sylvia somehow?'

'They might be in league with Gawain!' Clio pulled them over to the opposite side of the stage to the men. 'Just let me work out where the trapdoor is – we can get through it and out to the back of the stage. Then we can surprise Gawain.'

'What's he so angry about, anyway?'

Jeanie kept her voice low. 'Well, I overheard him saying that he just wanted her to listen. So that might fit with her... with her being his mum?'

Clio thought for a moment. 'Gawain?'

'Yes.'

'But they're so different.'

'Sure.' Jeanie sounded unusually confident. 'But he's the right age – fifty-ish. And maybe he's somehow found out that she's his mum. And so he went to her, expecting a big, lovely mum hug, and got told to bugger off. So he got angry, and tried to kill her?' She clicked her fingers. 'That would make sense, wouldn't it?'

'Yes. It fits!' Amber's voice dropped an octave. As someone whose own mum had abandoned her when she was just a baby, Clio knew Amber would understand how that might feel.

'So, is it Gawain? Is he her abandoned child?'

'I am.' A chilling voice came from behind them.

They all turned around, at the same time as Gawain shone a very bright torch into their faces.

'Gawain?'

'Yes, it's me.' He kept the light on them, steady and painfully bright. 'The hapless props man? Or the disastrous set designer? Take your pick.' He gave a high-pitched laugh that chilled Clio to the bone. 'And no, I cannot believe it either – it's so much more fun being centre stage than being one of the invisible crew, isn't it?' He opened his mouth, emitting a light tenor. 'We wish you a merry Christmas, we wish you a merry Christmas, we wish you a merry Christmas and a murderous New Year.'

Clio walked straight towards him, or rather to where she thought he was. But suddenly the torch was gone and her hands closed around thin air.

'Over here, darling.' His voice taunted her from somewhere to her left. 'Keep up, Clio. I'm not quite as useless as everyone thinks, now, am I?'

'Apparently not.' Clio was trying to track him but it was impossible in the inky blackness. She retreated back to her friends, her hands sliding into theirs. She needed them beside her. She felt stronger with her family around her.

'I've got Beatrice's blood in me, don't I?' Gawain's voice now boomed from the front of the stage. 'Like mother, like abandoned son.' A light flickered behind them and they turned, only to whirl around again as a beam of torchlight shone to their left. It illuminated Dexter, Ross and Kylie, who all had their arms around each other, looking terrified. With the light shining on them they sprang apart, trying to look cool and calm and failing miserably.

Clio stood her ground. 'Why are you trapping us here, Gawain?'

'So you can't tell the world what I've done.'

'Which is…?'

'I didn't kill her.' His voice cracked. 'I really, really didn't. I just wanted to make her see. I just wanted her to acknowledge everything I was to her, to let me get close to her, to build a real relationship. I just wanted her to let me hug her, but she wouldn't give me an inch. She just stood there, hating me, refusing to listen, even though I sneaked a DNA test by using a sample from one of her lipsticks.' He laughed. 'But, when I went to her dressing room on opening night, ready for a big reunion, all I got for my trouble was her trying to kick me out, the bitch.'

He was ranting now, unaware that Amber was now propelling Jeanie and Clio forward towards the sound of his voice. 'She was just so cold.' He sounded insane now, the whites of his eyes gleaming in the darkness. 'And then, just when I was getting very angry, understandably so I think, given that I had all the evidence I needed of who she was to me, of how she was my mother, I found I had my hands around her neck. But I wasn't going to kill her. I never meant to kill her. But she just – fell. And it was my fault. And so, I ran. That was how I left things with her. And the next thing I knew, she had been shot. She had faked her death to get rid of me and someone else killed her instead.

'And there's just no point any more.' Gawain was still going, his voice booming out across the stage. 'I've spent years waiting for her to acknowledge me, and now she's gone. So I can't let any of you leave. Because you know what I did. I tried to kill my own mother. I tried to get her to face up to the truth and she just didn't care. And now, as her only remaining relative, I need to build her legacy, to make this theatre great again, and I can't do that from behind bars. So now I have to kill you all too.' It sounded like he was crying now.

Clio nudged her friends. 'This way.' She started pushing them to the right. She had finally had an idea. Something useful they could do to save themselves.

'Why?' Amber didn't sound convinced.

'Trust me.' Clio squeezed her hand. She reached out her right foot and checked that they were in position. Then she pressed a switch to her left and the stage lights came on. The emergency backup switch. For a moment everyone stood still, blinking, unable to see. Then they all began to run. Gawain was heading straight for Clio, sprinting, his mouth set in a grimace. And then he was rugby tackled by Jeanie, and slammed to the ground, with Amber holding firmly on to that bloody cable-knit jumper as he tried to get away.

'Well done, Jeanie!' Clio sprinted past her. Jeanie tied Gawain's hands behind his back and sat on his torso.

'He's not going anywhere.' She smiled happily.

'Now get Dexter.' Amber yelled to be heard over Gawain's sobbing. 'GET HIM NOW!'

Clio was only too pleased to comply. It was Christmas on Sunday. She wanted to drink Baileys in her pyjamas and open presents on the sofa and hug Nina and take the piss out of Bez and overdose on roast potatoes. She didn't want be lying dead in an abandoned theatre, murdered by a rampaging set designer with an annoying jumper.

Clio wanted to live. Clio wanted to eat too many Quality Street and caterwaul carols at the telly. She didn't know why Amber wanted them to get Dexter, but she would do it anyway. She trusted Amber. No matter what.

The three of them ran at Dexter, but he pulled something out of his pocket. A shiny silver pistol. 'Don't you come near me!' He pointed it at them. 'Or I'll shoot!'

30

BEATRICE BUTLER

19.23: Two minutes until her death

Gawain had thought he was in charge when he had tried to strangle her, but fortunately for Beatrice he didn't have a clue how the human body actually worked.

Luckily, Beatrice had played enough death scenes to know how to fake it, so she had collapsed to the chaise-longue way before she had actually run short of air. She had heard Gawain's gasp, his footsteps leaving the room and then running down the corridor. Then she had sat up, rubbing her hand over her painful neck, and carried on getting ready for the show.

He wouldn't trouble her again, she was sure of that.

She had congratulated herself, as she did her make-up. She had done it. She had seen off her biggest mistake. Her son. Pretending to die had been a masterstroke, if she did say so herself. She still had her old magic. She could still hold her head high.

Beatrice Butler had no son. Never had, never would.

She was just about to stand up when she realised that the door was opening again. And the face that she saw was an unwelcome one, even more so when he pulled a pistol out of his pocket. She waited, meeting his eyes in the mirror, standing and turning towards him.

Beatrice Butler had come face to face with many pistols in her time, but the weapon had never had mistletoe and tinsel wrapped around the trigger before. She stared down the barrel, which was shaking violently, as was the entire body of the person who appeared to want her dead.

Beatrice felt an unfamiliar pulse of fear as she sat on her chaise-longue at gunpoint. She may have underestimated the risks she was taking. She may have played with fire. She had assumed that her companion was too feeble, too lacking in backbone, and too stupid to ever confront her face to face. Then she felt relief washing through her. The weapon trained on her chest was a prop gun, not a real one. A Christmas cracker would be a more effective murder weapon than this.

The clock was ticking though, so it was time to move things along. This wasn't her time to die, not yet. When the stage legend that was Beatrice Butler shed her mortal coil, she wouldn't be doing so while wearing a fairy costume, her stage make-up only half done, her legacy not yet certain. No. She needed just a few more hours. One night to make stage history.

She stood up, smiling at her would-be killer, daring them to shoot. She used her most commanding tones, the rounded vowels that had captivated audiences around the world for the past fifty years. 'Don't be silly, now.' She held her hand out, her ruby ring sparkling. 'Give me the gun.'

'Give me the ring.' The pistol was veering right and left now. Beatrice saw the letters engraved on the barrel and her heart started to race. She hadn't been mistaken, had she? Her eyesight wasn't what it was.

Sweat dripped down the face of her assailant. 'You need to do what I tell you. The ring. Now.'

Beatrice pulled herself up to her full height. 'I am Beatrice Butler. I never do what I am told.'

Then she lunged forward and reached for the gun.

31

AMBER

Dexter waved his pistol around, indicating that they should all congregate in the corner of the stage. Amber hadn't expected this. She had followed her gut, asking Clio and Jeanie to capture him. She had simply followed the clues: Dexter had the ring in his dressing room and had gambling debts, so he had probably been involved in her death. The pistol that had been used to shoot Beatrice must be firmly in a police evidence bag, locked away by Marco's team. Did Dexter have a spare? Was this weapon a real threat?

It seemed unlikely. But Amber came to a halt, and obeyed his instructions, the bright stage lights making it impossible to hide. She wondered if the pistol had any bullets in it. It looked old, possibly a prop, but she couldn't take the chance. She needed to get everyone else behind her.

She waved her friends backwards, taking one step forward herself. Clio and Jeanie melted into the background, and she could only hope that they stayed there. She took a deep breath.

'Gawain.'

'Yes?' The man was cowering at the back, his hands raised above his head, all his earlier bravado gone.

'Was Beatrice wearing her ring when you left her dressing room?'

Gawain nodded. 'Yes.'

'QUIET.' Dexter wasn't quite quick enough to stop Gawain's answer. 'ALL OF YOU, BE QUIET.'

The pistol was wobbling all over the place now. Dexter's face was pale, his eyes wild.

Amber held her hands up. 'Listen, Dexter, we know that you killed Beatrice. Everyone else tried, mind you. But you were the one who did it. But you didn't kill her because you hated her, like everyone else. You just did it to get the ring, didn't you? If it was on her finger when Gawain left her, and I have no reason to disbelieve him, given that we found it in his dressing room, then you must have been the one who took it. So there's no point fighting this, is there? Not really. You had the ring. And you killed her to get it.'

Dexter was still holding on to the pistol, aiming it right at Amber. 'No. You're wrong.'

'Am I?' Amber took a step towards him. 'How?'

She passed Ross, who had thrown himself down on the ground, appearing to have given up hope, whimpering quietly about how he'd give up his shady life and go and do good deeds for charity for the rest of his days. Clio and Amber were silent, watching him.

Dexter spoke slowly, so quiet that Amber could barely hear him. 'I didn't mean to do it.'

'Didn't mean to what?' Amber took another step.

'I didn't mean to kill her!' A muscle flickered in Dexter's cheek. 'I didn't know it was a real gun. I just picked it up from the props table! I just wanted to scare her, to get her to hand the ring over so I could pay off my debts. I'm not a bad guy!'

Amber took one more step, watching him carefully.

'And then, she lunged for the gun, and so I fired out of surprise and...' He put a hand to his mouth. 'There was so much blood. Oh my God, so much blood! I still can't believe what I did. Why was there a real gun on the props table? Why?'

Amber almost felt sorry for him. Almost.

'And there was nothing I could do. She was gone. And I'd done it. And so, I just, panicked. I took the ring. I just – well, I did it automatically, really. Then I wiped the pistol down...' He was struggling for breath. 'To remove my fingerprints, and I ran. There was no blood on my costume, somehow, so I just went straight to the wings, and nobody noticed. But all the time I just had this image of her in my head, lying there, dead, and knowing that I'd done it!'

Amber took another step. He was too far gone to notice.

'And I didn't know the gun was real.' He focused on Amber, seeing for the first time how close she was. 'You must believe me.'

Amber spoke slowly, holding his gaze. 'I do believe you. And if you give me this gun then we can all get out of here.'

'No.' Dexter narrowed his eyes at her. 'No, I won't give it to you.'

She held out her hand. 'You know it's for the best.'

'No.'

'You're not going to shoot me, Dexter.'

'Yes, I am, if you don't get away from me.' He was now aiming at her forehead.

It wasn't real, Amber was sure of it. But she held up her hands. 'What's your plan here, Dexter? What are you aiming at? To intentionally murder someone this time? In front of a room full of witnesses? Is that really the answer here?'

'I just want you to let me leave. I deserve that.'

He deserved nothing of the sort. He deserved to spend several years in a cell at His Majesty's pleasure.

'Then...' She took another step forward, only for Dexter to suddenly disappear. The pistol flew from his hands and landed with a clatter at Amber's feet.

'YES.' Clio clapped her hands triumphantly and patted the long black lever to her right. 'I did it. The trapdoor worked! He's down there! We got him.'

From beneath the stage they could hear him ranting and raving as the trapdoor closed above him.

Jeanie stepped forward. 'But he can escape through to the back of the theatre.'

'Oh no, he can't!' Melissa marched onto the stage from the back, a key in her hand. 'Because me and that hottie, Marco, just locked the door.'

'Melissa. You're okay.' Amber took a step towards her.

'Yeah, sis, of course I'm okay.' Melissa smiled. 'Be careful there, you look like you might be about so show some emotion.'

Amber shook her head, blinking a tear away. 'No. I don't do that.'

'Are you sure?' Melissa arched her eyebrows. 'I'll have you in a Christmas jumper yet, my friend!'

'Never.' Amber reached out and hugged Jeanie and Clio.

'Me too?' Melissa pressed her palms together, as if in prayer.

'Oh, come on then. Get in here.' Amber rolled her eyes, hiding quite how relieved she was that her half-sister was okay. 'If you must.' Then she pulled away as police officers started to spread out across the stage, arresting the other members of the cast for the attempted murder of Beatrice Butler.

'Hang on...' Amber's eyes met Jeanie's. 'Does this mean we don't need to be Daisy the Cow any more?'

Clio shook her head. 'Absolutely not. Though given how many of the cast are going to be arrested, you might even have speaking parts too. We can reopen the theatre after Christmas, maybe, with a new, potted panto show. A minimal cast. Lots of costume changes. It'll be great!'

Amber and Jeanie groaned.

'I'll be in it!' Melissa beamed. 'Wow, I'm such a Brit nowadays! First the Mistletoe Murder Club, now a panto star!'

Amber sighed. 'One step at a time, Melissa.'

'Ahhh, you old misery.' Melissa kissed her on the cheek. 'You love me really.'

And Amber had to admit, just to herself of course, that maybe, just maybe, that was true.

32

CLIO

'God, does she ever stop singing?' Jeanie reached for the bottle of red wine in the middle of the table and filled up her glass. She arched her eyebrows inquiringly at Clio, who nodded enthusiastically. Jeanie dutifully filled up her glass too.

Clio looked over to where Bez's girlfriend Tiara was drying up the first of many roasting tins, while simultaneously blasting out 'Feliz Navidad' at full volume.

'That's nothing.' She frowned, as she tried again to use the nutcracker that defeated her every single year. 'The whole caravan park can hear her in the mornings, though obviously it's worse for me as I'm next door to Bez. I got all the residents of the caravan park ear-plugs for Christmas. Bez was annoyed with me, but everyone else was thrilled.'

Nina sank down onto the bench to her left. 'I may never move again.' She patted her tummy. 'I should not have had that last bit of Christmas pudding. Why do I never learn?'

Clio put her arm around her daughter's shoulders. Given half a chance, she would surgically attach herself to Nina and never let her go back to university ever again, but as her daughter wasn't keen on this version of her future, she was confining herself to enormous amounts of hugs while she was here for the holidays.

'You never learn because you're my daughter.' Clio shrugged. 'Look at me, thinking Ross was my friend, while all the time he was a crazy would-be killer.'

Nina grimaced. 'Well, so was everyone else in the cast and the crew. Except you. Go you!'

Clio grinned. 'Yes. Go me. Let's toast my amazingness with more wine!'

Nina considered for a second, her head on one side, brown eyes sparkling. 'Ooh, go on then.' She held out her glass and Jeanie topped it up.

Clio looked at her friend, who was wearing a Santa hat pulled low over her forehead and some kind of Christmas tree outfit that had apparently been created by the twins as her Christmas present. It involved brown leggings and a green triangle top and on both of Jeanie's sleeves were golden bells that jangled every time she moved. She looked hot, sweaty and was coming out in a rash.

'Who wants to play Racing Santas?' Bez, Clio's ex and Nina's dad, looked hopefully around the crowded living room of his static caravan.

Silence.

Bez clasped his hands imploringly. 'Please?'

'Oh, go on then.' Jeanie's husband Tan stood up, his face nearly as red as his reindeer jumper.

'That's my man.' Bez clapped his hands together. He opened a shoebox that was on the side. 'Oh.' His face fell. 'Where are the Santas? They've gone!'

Jeanie groaned. 'Yumi. Jack!'

Tan was already looking for the twins. 'Found them! They're in the bathroom giving the Santas a bath!'

'Of course they are.' Jeanie rolled her eyes.

'We just need to towel the Santas off.' Tan walked back in with a twin under each arm, each clutching several small plastic Santas. 'Then they'll be ready to race, Bez!'

Tiara picked up another roasting tin, transitioning seamlessly to 'All I Want for Christmas.'

Nina widened her eyes. 'I think it's Baileys o'clock, don't you?' She leant closer. 'Either that, or I'm going to need some cotton wool.'

'YES.' Clio and Jeanie nodded as Tiara's voice soared higher. It was most definitely Baileys o'clock.

Nina got the bottle from the sideboard as Amber came over and joined them.

Her friend was looking unusually cheerful, which was surprising, given that

Melissa had persuaded her to wear a red Mistletoe Murder Club T-shirt. Jeanie the Christmas tree had been given a pass, but Clio was wearing hers too, as was Melissa, who was tucked away in the corner chatting away to Marco. She had brought him along without asking anyone, of course. No wonder Amber was laying into the red wine.

Clio took a sip of hers. 'Why are you on your phone again, Amber?'

'I'm just checking my messages. Did you know the publicity from us catching the panto killer means that we now have even more of a waiting list? We're booked up until 2026!'

'Amber.' Clio groaned and threw her favourite North Pole This Way cushion at her friend. 'It's Christmas Day. Can't you stop working, just for a minute? Please?'

'Not when things are looking this good!'

Clio rolled her eyes at her friend's workaholic tendencies, while simultaneously feeling an inner wave of satisfaction. Apprehending a celebrity like Dexter Buchanan had proved an incredibly good move during the traditional Christmas news lull, helped by a famous trio of comedians doing a reconstruction of the pantomime chase scene involving mistletoe, an angry Santa and Dexter as the villain. It went viral, and now Clio, Amber, Melissa and Jeanie were widely known as The Mistletoe Murder Club. The other members of the cast were all behind bars as well, awaiting trial. Even Sylvia and Jaxon had confessed to leaving Beatrice the poisoned mince pie because she had ruined Jaxon's book and Sylvia's Hollywood moment.

Life was good, Clio reflected, apart from Tiara's bloody singing. She watched Bez, noting the glances he was giving his girlfriend, wondering if they were as happy as he professed. She would talk to him later, get to the truth. She was good at that, apparently. Meanwhile, she hugged her daughter even closer, risking the groan that inevitably came. Bez was joking with Tan as he set up the Santas, and Clio felt a tug that she didn't really understand. She and Bez didn't belong together. Did they?

She realised Nina was watching her. 'What is it, Mum?'

'Nothing.' Clio shook her head. 'Just...'

Nina leant close. 'Mum. We all know you're jealous of Tiara.'

Clio shook her head. 'Jealous! I'm not jealous. Not at all.'

Nina stared at Amber and Jeanie and raised her eyebrows. 'Told you she was in denial.'

'I'm not in denial!'

The three of them started laughing. 'Sure, you're not.' Amber picked up a party blower decorated with Christmas puddings and blew it in Clio's face. 'That's why you're staring at them all the time.'

'Not all the time!' Clio felt herself start to smile. Bez did seem to be working out nowadays – his red 'Dear Santa – Define Good' T-shirt clung to what appeared to be actual abs, and his forearms were bulging. She caught his eye, smiled and looked away. This wasn't the Bez that Clio knew. The Bez she knew was normally to be found horizontal on the sofa with a beer and his guitar.

Tiara took a break from her constant karaoke and left the caravan and Clio got to her feet.

'Need any help with those Santas, Bez?'

He widened his eyes. 'I'm sorry. Are you Clio Lawrence?'

She nodded. 'I hope so. Though I have had a few drinks, so I may not be firing on all cylinders.'

'But Clio Lawrence never, ever offers to help.' He smiled down at her and she felt a thread tighten between them.

'Like I said, I've had a few drinks.'

Bez grinned and flipped his reindeer Santa glasses down onto his nose. 'Baileys? Your lifeblood?'

'No.' Clio tapped him playfully on the arm. 'Margaritas are my lifeblood; Baileys is Christmas in a glass.'

He put an arm around her shoulders, and she leant against him, enjoying his solid familiarity. 'So it is. I remember you puking your guts up on our first Christmas together. Do you remember?'

Clio shuddered. 'I remember you totally failing to hold my hair back, yes.'

'Lies, all lies.' Bez shook his head.

Nina was shouting something across to them both.

Clio cupped her hand to her ear. 'What?'

'You're under the mistletoe.' Nina's eyes snapped with mischief above the Christmas pudding pyjamas she had owned since she was a teenager.

'So?' As Clio said it, her eyes met Bez's, and for a moment it was just the two of them, face to face, Christmas T-shirt to Christmas T-shirt. For a minute they hovered, then, 'I'm back' came a trill from the door and Tiara re-entered the caravan.

Clio sighed, and walked back around, squeezing her way past the twins, to join her friends and her daughter.

'Never mind, Mum.' Nina's hand crept into hers. 'He and Tiara won't last long – she doesn't like his guitar playing. It's doomed.'

'I...'

Nina shook her head. 'Mum. I know you better than you know yourself on this one, believe me.'

'She really does.' Amber leant across and nabbed a cold roast potato from the plate in the middle of the table. 'Nice mince pies, by the way.'

Clio shook her head. 'Liar. I caught Bez using one to prop the table up earlier.'

'I guess you'd better stick to directing, hey?'

'Maybe I should.' Clio felt a surge of excitement. With everyone else behind bars, there really was only one candidate to take over from Beatrice Butler as director of the Christmas pantomime. She had left the theatre to the amateur dramatic society in her will, and Clio knew that next year's production would be better than ever, under her stewardship.

The only question was whether she could get Amber and Jeanie back as the pantomime cow. She sat back and sipped her Baileys. She had a year to persuade them. They didn't stand a chance.

***

MORE FROM KATIE MARSH

Katie Marsh's next title is available to pre-order now here: https://mybook.to/KatieMarshBook5BackAd

ACKNOWLEDGEMENTS

Thank you to my readers everywhere for choosing this book! I am so grateful to every single one of you. Thank you to my wonderful agent Charlie Campbell, the best champion an author could ever have, and to my brilliant editor, Isobel Akenhead, whose notes bring out the best in every book I write.

I am so grateful to Marcela Torres for promoting my work with such skill and creativity. I am very lucky to work with the wider Boldwood team – Wendy Neale, Isabelle Flynn, Claire Fenby, Hayley Russell, Ben Wilson, and Grace Cooper who are so brilliant at what they do – thank you for putting the word out there about my books. Huge thanks to Debra Newhouse and Gary Jukes for their eagle-eyed edits.

I am so grateful to Isabelle Broom and my writer crew – long may we word race and share panicky WhatsApps about plots and structural edits. And thank you to my amazing mum and dad, to my inspirational big brother and to my local gang: Robynn Hyde, Roz Orchard, Helen Thirlway, Tamara Bathgate – I love you all.

And finally, to Max, Evie and Aidan: you are the best Christmas companions I could ever wish for, and I can't wait to play 'Racing Santa' with you this year. I am going to win, obviously, so don't get any ideas.

ABOUT THE AUTHOR

Katie Marsh wrote five romantic fiction novels before turning to crime. Her debut, 'My Everything' was a World Book night pick, and her books are published across ten countries. She lives in the English countryside with her family and loves coffee, puzzles and pretending she is in charge of her children. Her move into crime was inspired by her own bumpy arrival into midlife, complete with insomnia so severe that she once forgot her own name. Her crime debut 'How Not to Murder your Ex', was inspired by the friendships that helped her to get back on track.

Missing Clio, Amber and Jeanie? Sign up for Katie Marsh's newsletter to read the FREE short story, The Disco Detectives!

Visit Katie's website: www.katie-marsh.com

Follow Katie on social media here:

facebook.com/katiemarshauthor
instagram.com/katiemarshauthor

ABOUT THE AUTHOR

Katie Marsh wrote five romantic fiction novels before turning to crime. Her debut, My Everything, was a World Book Night pick, and her books are published in seven countries. She lives in the Brighton countryside with her family and loves coffee, puzzles and pretending she is fit. Like other fifty-five-year-olds, her move into crime was inspired by her own (rarely acted upon) desire to complete with insouciance so severe that she once forgot her own name. Her current debut 'How Not to Murder Your Ex', was inspired by the friendships that help cheer us all back on track.

Minus Bo, Amber and Jemima, of course, Katie Marsh never stops reading the BBC Shipping News The Cake Date aloud.

Visit Katie's website: www.katie-marsh.com

Follow Katie on social media here

ALSO BY KATIE MARSH

The Bad Girls Detective Agency Series

How Not To Murder Your Ex

Murder on the Dancefloor

Murder on the Menu

The Mistletoe Murder Club

POISON
& pens

POISON & PENS IS THE HOME OF
COZY MYSTERIES SO POUR YOURSELF
A CUP OF TEA & GET SLEUTHING!

DISCOVER PAGE-TURNING NOVELS FROM
YOUR FAVOURITE AUTHORS &
MEET NEW FRIENDS

JOIN OUR
FACEBOOK GROUP

BIT.LY/POISONANDPENSFB

SIGN UP TO OUR
NEWSLETTER

BIT.LY/POISONANDPENSNEWS

Boldwood

Boldwood Books is an award-winning fiction publishing company seeking out the best stories from around the world.

Find out more at www.boldwoodbooks.com

Join our reader community for brilliant books, competitions and offers!

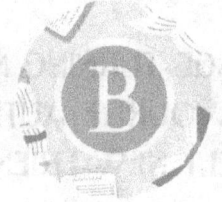

Follow us
@BoldwoodBooks
@TheBoldBookClub

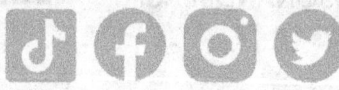

Sign up to our weekly deals newsletter

https://bit.ly/BoldwoodBNewsletter

www.ingramcontent.com/pod-product-compliance
Lightning Source LLC
Chambersburg PA
CBHW011404210526
45464CB00009B/3035